Level F

Columbus, OH

Photo Credits

10–11 ©Maurice Faulk/SuperStock; 34 file photo; 76–77 ©PhotoDisc/Getty Images, Inc.; 77 (t)Library of Congress; 77 (b) ©Klaus Hackenberg/zefa/Corbis; 94 courtesy of Iza Trapani; 102 (t)file photo; 102 (b)Courtesy of HK Portfolio; 128 (t) ©Duomo/CORBIS; 128 (b)Courtesy of Carol Thompson; 136–137 ©David Muench/CORBIS; 138 ©David Aubrey/CORBIS; 139 ©Erika Craddock/Photo Researchers, Inc.; 166, 192 file photo; 194–195 ©Angelo Cavalli/zefa/CORBIS; 196 ©Fridmar Damm/zefa/Corbis; 197 ©Ted Levin; 222 (t) courtesy of Susan Blackaby; 222 (b) courtesy of Charlene DeLage; 224—225 ©Randy Wells/Getty Images, Inc.; 225 ©Leonard Rue Enterprises/Animals Animals/Earth Scenes; 226 ©PhotoDisc/Getty Images, Inc.; 227 ©Keren Su/CORBIS; 228–229 (bkgd) ©Matt Brown/CORBIS; 230 ©Nancy Rotenberg; 231 ©Dwight R. Kuhn; 232 ©Greg Ryan/Sally Beyer; 233 ©PhotoDisc/Getty Images, Inc.; 234 ©Nancy Rotenberg; 235 ©Peter Smithers/CORBIS; 236 ©Jay Ireland & Georgienne E. Bradley/Bradleyireland.com; 237 ©Michael K. Nichols/National Geographic Image Collection; 238 (inset) ©Christopher Knight/Science Photo Library; 238 (bkgd) ©Jane Burton/Bruce Coleman, Inc.; 239 (t) ©Nancy Rotenbery; 239 (b) ©Ed Reschke; 240 ©Britstock/Cheryl Hogue; 241 ©Joy Spurr/Bruce Coleman, Inc.; 242 ©Dwight R. Kuhn; 243 ©Rick Wetherbee; 244 ©Joe McDonald/McDonald Wildlife Photography; 245 © David Cavagnaro/Visuals Unlimited; 246–247 ©Keren Su/CORBIS.

SRAonline.com

Copyright © 2008 by SRA/McGraw-Hill.

All rights reserved. No part of this publication may be reproduced or distributed in any form or by any means, or stored in a database or retrieval system, without the prior written consent of The McGraw-Hill Companies, Inc., including, but not limited to, network storage or transmission, or broadcast for distance learning.

Printed in the United States of America.

Send all inquiries to:
SRA/McGraw-Hill
4400 Easton Commons
Columbus, OH 43219-6188

ISBN: 978-0-07-608876-8
MHID: 0-07-608876-6

1 2 3 4 5 6 7 8 9 QWV 13 12 11 10 08 07

Unit Themes

Unit 1 — Hang In There

Unit 2 — Legend Has It

Unit 3 — From Head to Toe

Unit 4 — Charting a Course

Unit 5 — To the Beat

Unit 6 — Pastimes

Table of Contents

Unit 1 — Hang In There

Wilderness Lessons 2
   by Monique Williams
   illustrated by Ralph Canaday

John Wesley Powell: Brains and Grit 10
   by Jennifer Wright

Making a Difference 16
   by José Gilberto
   illustrated by Jack Pennington

The Claim 22
   by Myra Smith
   illustrated by Cheryl Kirk Noll

A Very Proper Hero 30
   by Thaddeus Gibson

Maya's Dream 36
   by Richard Shannon
   illustrated by Carol Newsom

Getting Ready to Win 42
   by Sandra Liatsos
   illustrated by Ken Tiessen

Poetry Reflections 43
Reading Reflections 44

Table of Contents

Unit 2 — Legend Has It

To Celebrate the New Year 46
a Japanese folktale retold by Pamela Haskins
illustrated by Phyllis P. Cahill

Arachne's Web 54
a Greek myth retold by Felipe Salgado
illustrated by Janet Nelson

Chinese History, One Story at a Time 60
by Heather Vance

The Frog Kingdom 66
a Native American Tlingit legend retold by Liza Cho
illustrated by Christy Hale

A World of Tricksters 72
by Marcos Mata

The Sharing of Gifts 78
a Jewish folktale, based on "The Magic Pomegranate," retold by Avi Lublin
illustrated by Julie Downing

Dragon's Advantage 86
by Audrey B. Baird
illustrated by Tom Price

Poetry Reflections 87
Reading Reflections 88

Table of Contents

Unit 3 — From Head to Toe

The Skeleton—Top to Bottom 90
by Darius Jackson

Can You Hear Me? 96
by Elizabeth Watson
illustrated by Geoff Smith

What's That Smell? 104
by Carlota Diaz

Graduation Day 110
by Judith Chen
illustrated by Marcy Ramsey

More Than Meets the Eye 116
by Sunrise Jones

From Food to Fuel 122
by Vivek Kumar

Ouch! 128
by Ann Dixon
illustrated by Mark Schroder

Poetry Reflections 129
Reading Reflections 130

Table of Contents

Unit 4 — Charting a Course

The Great Navigators . . . And the Greatest 132
by Harold Wu

Strangers on the Horizon 138
by Marta Leal
illustrated by Roberta C. Morales

Just Who Were These Vikings? 144
by Marcus Fyle
illustrated by Denny Bond

The Seven Voyages of Zheng He 152
by Helen Forrest

Sauerkraut, the Secret to Sailing Success.....................158
by Matt Bernél
illustrated by Jim Spence

My Travels with Marco Polo 166
by Treyvon Grant
illustrated by Lindy Burnett

Maps 174
by Dorothy Brown Thompson
illustrated by Jesse Reisch

Poetry Reflections 175
Reading Reflections 176

Table of Contents

Unit 5: To the Beat

Mariachi! 178
    by Stan Martin

Blue Kentucky 182
    by Shelly Porter
    illustrated by Bradley Clark

The Swans of the Bolshoi 188
    by Melanie Sabato
    illustrated by Johanna Van der Sterre

Island Homecoming 194
    by Alma Lazo
    illustrated by Stacy Schuett

Satchmo: One of a Kind 200
    by Mara Loveland

A Musical Connection 208
    by Mohit Bhatti

Danse Africaine 214
    by Langston Hughes
    illustrated by Chris van Es

Poetry Reflections 215
Reading Reflections 216

Table of Contents

Unit 6 Pastimes

The Very Best Sport 218
 by Camilla York
 illustrated by Paula Zinnegrabe Wendland

Spice Up Your Day 226
 by Ian Trevor

Mexico: A Study in Contrasts 232
 by Garrett McTavish

Touring the Amsterdam Canal 238
 by Sophie Millet
 illustrated by Marcy Ramsey

Tea with Friends 244
 by Dorothea Nixon

Brazil's Big Party 248
 by Justin Blanco

African Night 252
 by Susan Scott Sutton
 illustrated by Ken Perkins

Poetry Reflections 253
Reading Reflections 254
Glossary 256

Focus Questions How does Alejandro find the strength to keep going? How do you motivate yourself when things get difficult?

Wilderness Lessons

by Monique Williams
illustrated by Ralph Canaday

Alejandro looked at the camping gear spread on the floor. "I have to carry all this stuff on my back?" he asked.

"You bet," said Rico. "This is a ten-day trek. I sent all the trip information pamphlets to you, right?" It was true. Rico had mailed him a stack of information about this hike in the Colorado Rockies. "Let me guess. You didn't even read it, right?"

Alejandro shrugged and grinned. Rico sighed. "Well, at least you got some good boots," he said.

Alejandro held up a foot and admired his new hiking boots. "Yes, these boots are going to take me places," he said.

"Well, you still have to hike there—with all that gear on your back," Rico joked.

The next morning, Rico and Alejandro gathered with the rest of the group at a trailhead high on a remote mountain road. Rico was a group leader, along with a tall college student named Sonia, who had been making this trek for years.

"Short day today," said Sonia, shouldering her pack. "We'll hike seven miles and set up camp at Sweet Meadow."

Alejandro headed up the trail feeling confident and excited. After all, he was an accomplished athlete; he played football and tennis. Things went fine for the first mile, but then the hikers came to a stretch of trail that ascended narrow switchbacks over a ridge. About halfway up, Alejandro was completely out of breath and leaned against a rock wall, panting.

Rico stopped. "How's it going?" he asked.

"Whew! We haven't gone far. Why is it so hard to climb?" Alejandro asked, huffing.

"Elevation," said Rico. "We are eight thousand feet above sea level right now, and the air gets thinner the higher you go. It was all in the information pamphlets . . . ."

"Okay, okay, I guess I should have looked them over." Alejandro heaved himself upright again.

When Alejandro finally reached Sweet Meadow with some other struggling hikers, the group had set up camp.

"That first day is a real challenge," said Sonia. "You think you're in shape until you try hauling fifty pounds of gear at this elevation. It takes some getting used to."

"Oh, I am feeling just fine," Alejandro claimed. He did not want to seem weak. The group ate a quick dinner and got ready for bed.

"Twelve miles tomorrow, everyone," said Rico.

   The next morning, Alejandro's legs were so stiff he could barely hobble out of the tent. He could not believe how much his knees and calves ached and throbbed. For the first time he doubted he had the tenacity to complete this trek.
   Rico saw his friend shuffle slowly to the campfire. "Don't worry too much, Alejandro. You'll feel better when we get going."
   Miles one and two went by fairly well, but then the climbing began. Before he knew it, Alejandro was gasping in the thin air. He had to stop and rest three times in half an hour. Alejandro's spirits sank as he again recalled that no sport had ever challenged him like this did. What if he could not make it on this trip? As Alejandro staggered into the lunch camp, he decided to talk to Rico.

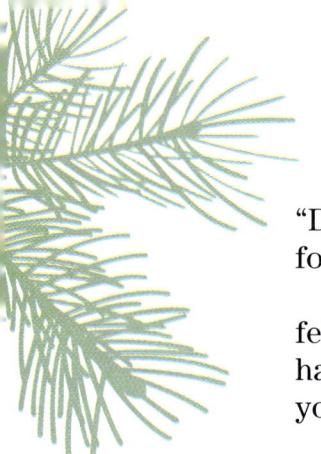

"I don't know about this," he said to Rico in a low voice. "Do you think I should just turn around before I make a fool of myself?"

Rico shook his head. "You're not the first person who has felt this way, Alejandro. Even a really good athlete can get hammered by the elevation up here. Just hang in there, and you'll feel better eventually."

The rest of the day did not get any easier—in fact, it was brutal. Every time Alejandro had to stop and rest, a voice in his head would tell him to quit, but then another voice would pipe in and make him keep moving. Finally, after twelve long miles, Alejandro limped into camp, heaved off his pack, and joined the group by the campfire.

"Way to go, Alejandro," said Sonia. "I'm impressed you're sticking with it."

Later, Rico helped Alejandro dress the blisters on his feet for the next day. "Even great boots need to be broken in when they're new," he said. "Remember the sports gear guidelines I sent you . . . . Oh, never mind," Rico said, shaking his head.

7

The next day the group covered ten miles. Alejandro still felt sore and short of breath, but maybe not quite as much. He even glanced around at the picturesque surroundings. "Wow, this really is extraordinary," he thought as he watched a herd of elk move through the valley below.

Every day Alejandro felt a little better. He could hike faster, and he did not have to contemplate every step he was taking. On day six the group planned to scale Storm King, a fourteen-thousand-foot peak.

"Ready for this, Alejandro?" Rico asked.

"I think so," said Alejandro. "I went through the checklist a few times, but ultimately I'm just going to pace myself."

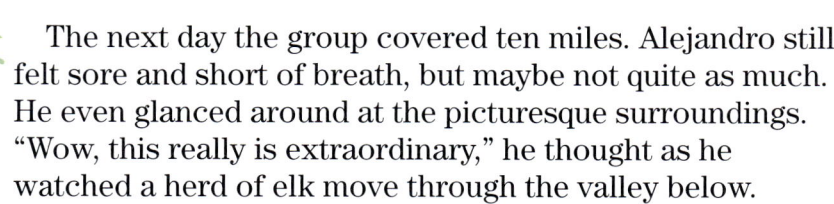

"That's the only way to do it, friend," said Rico. "You have to respect the wilderness. It's a place where you can learn some things about yourself."

"I definitely feel like I've been through some wilderness lessons," said Alejandro. "Now let's see what Storm King has to teach us."

Focus Questions How did John Wesley Powell distinguish himself? What drove him to explore the Grand Canyon?

John Wesley Powell: Brains and Grit

by Jennifer Wright

Who was John Wesley Powell? To many who knew him, he was a brilliant young man.

During his Illinois boyhood in the 1840s and 1850s, teachers were few, so Powell had to make nature his classroom. He went about collecting shells, minerals, and other natural objects and studied them by himself. He made long trips to learn more. Once he rowed the entire length of the Ohio River. He also walked through parts of Wisconsin, Iowa, and Missouri, studying the land and its creatures.

By age twenty-two, Powell knew so much that the Illinois Natural History Society elected him to its board. He never graduated from college, but a few years later he became a college professor. He also gave public lectures on scientific subjects and later was given honorary advanced degrees from Harvard and a university in Germany. Those who thought Powell was a "brain" were right!

But others knew a very different John Wesley Powell. They saw a tough, gritty man who feared nothing. When the Civil War broke out, Powell enlisted and fought in many battles. In one, he lost his right arm. But as soon as he healed, he went back and fought some more. Later he needed a second painful operation. After the operation, now with the rank of major, he went right back into battle.

After the war, these two John Wesley Powells—the smart and the brave—became one. In 1869 he decided to do what no one else had ever dared: He would travel the length of the Grand Canyon by boat.

The Colorado River cut through the canyon. Native Americans called it a river of death. For hundreds of years, people had set off on its boiling, raging waters—never to be seen again.

The Grand Canyon is about a mile deep in some places. The inquisitive Powell wanted to find out how it was formed. So he drew up plans for sturdy boats made of solid oak. Then he found nine brave men for a crew. On May 24, they pushed off from shore on the Green River, which flowed into the Colorado.

Soon they reached a set of rapids—the first of hundreds they would face. The current was so swift they could hardly steer. Again and again they plunged over steep falls. The boats were battered by huge boulders. If not for their watertight compartments, the boats would have been swamped. The men could only hang on for dear life!

But once they were on the river, there was no turning back. Day after day, Powell and his men traveled, never knowing what lay around the next bend. The rapids smashed one boat to pieces. They lost most of the food they had brought along. Tired and hungry, the men took a dreadful beating.

After less than a month, one man said he was leaving. "I have had more excitement than a man deserves in a lifetime," he told Powell. Then he climbed out of the canyon. He reached a nearby settlement. But there his story ended. No one knows what became of him.

Meanwhile Powell and his crew pushed on. Besides the roaring rapids, the canyon held other dangers. Deadly snakes, scorpions, and spiders lived among the rocks on shore. Bears and mountain lions were all around. The desert heat could be terrible, and the nights were chilly.

Worst of all were flash floods. Miles upstream, a rainstorm would dump huge amounts of water into the Colorado River. Without warning, the river would rise suddenly. The men had to scramble to save the boats and avoid drowning.

Ignoring danger, Powell carried on his scientific work. Many mornings, before breakfast, he would climb to the highest place he could find to map the area and make other notes. One day he nearly lost his life when his foot slipped and he fell over the rim of the canyon. He grabbed on to a bush a few feet down. But with only one arm, he could not haul himself up. Hanging in space, he shouted to his crew. After several long minutes, a man came to help. But there was nothing long enough for him to reach Powell. Thinking quickly, he snatched up a pair of pants and held them down the canyon wall. Powell grabbed one of the legs and was pulled to safety.

   Two months later, three more men had had enough of this dangerous journey. At a place now called Separation Canyon, they begged Powell to abandon the river. But Powell held fast to his goal. The men said their good-byes and left. Only two days later, Powell and his remaining men saw some settlers fishing along the riverbank. Their amazing journey was over. They stumbled ashore, ragged and starved. One settler asked whether they were humans or only part of his imagination. For months no one had thought they would come out alive.
   Powell not only survived, but in 1871 he made the journey a *second* time. Then he lived thirty-one more years as a distinguished scientist, teacher, and writer. In every area of his life, he proved himself to be a man of brains and grit—and a man who never gave up.

Focus Questions How do these six friends make a difference? What can you do to help your community?

Making a Difference

by José Gilberto

illustrated by Jack Pennington

The six friends were eager to get to the park. Juana, Henry, Corine, Sunita, Kelly, and Miguel had been best pals since the first grade. They studied together, played sports together, and even worked on community projects together. The year before, they had raised money for a family in need. But now these six middle-school students were about to tackle their most challenging project yet.

The friends met for a quick game of touch football before dinner and homework. Juana flung the football high into the air, and Henry had to take several steps back to catch it.

"Hey, you're really improving. You never would have been able to throw like that last year," yelled Henry.

"Yes, I've been practicing. I bet you won't be able to catch this one." Juana threw the ball even farther into the park.

"Uh, oh," hollered Henry as he sprinted backward, "you've done it now. It's out of the park. I think it went in the yard of that abandoned house."

Juana saw the football in the front yard close to the empty brick two-story. As she rushed to grab it, she heard muffled noises from the direction of the backyard. She could hear the murmur of voices and . . . meowing! Juana crept to the side of the house and spied two men whispering to each other and hovering over something. They were huddling over a cat and three kittens!

The other five friends swiftly closed in behind Juana.

"Shhh," she whispered to the others as she held her finger to her lips. "Those two men are feeding the cats."

"Who are they?" asked Corine.

17

The friends must have been speaking too loudly. The startled men jumped and turned to face them. Kelly immediately recognized them as old friends of her parents. The two groups were shy at first, but Kelly gave brief introductions. The friends learned that the men lived at a nearby shelter. Weeks earlier, they had chanced upon this deserted house and the feral cat colony in the backyard. They had been concerned about the cats ever since.

"What are feral cats?" Kelly asked.

"Feral cats are wild cats who live outside without homes," responded Mr. Garcia, one of the two men. "Unfortunately, millions of stray cats and dogs roam our streets without homes of their own."

Mr. Daniels, the other man, added, "We've been caring for three families of cats. Whatever food we get at the shelter, we share with them."

The men walked the two miles to the house and back every day in order to feed and spend time with the cats. At the shelter, the men were given food and a place to sleep. They had counselors to talk to and even help them find jobs. But their biggest concern at the moment was the cat colony. Someone in the neighborhood had discovered them feeding the cats and wanted to dispose of the colony.

"What can we do?" asked Sunita. "The cats need you, and you need the cats."

"We wish more people felt as you do," said Mr. Garcia.

"I know who can help us," spoke up Miguel. "My mom started a petition in the neighborhood to start a recycling program. It was hard getting signatures, or names, at first. Most people just didn't want to bother. But eventually she got enough signatures and started the program."

"She persevered," stated Mr. Garcia.

Mr. Daniels asked, "Do you all know the meaning of *perseverance?*"

The friends shrugged.

"Perseverance is a quality people have when they continue to try to do something despite obstacles," said Mr. Daniels.

"Just like you," said Corine.

"And just like the cats," added Kelly.

In the weeks that followed, the six friends, along with their parents and other students from the school, started a campaign to save the cat colony. Mr. Garcia and Mr. Daniels had more supporters than they ever imagined. The local humane society got involved by supplying some food for the cats, building igloo homes for the coming winter, and starting a spay-and-neuter program for the colony. The society even found part-time jobs for both men.

"I like that word *perseverance*," stated Juana one afternoon, shortly after Mr. Garcia and Mr. Daniels had started their jobs. The whole group of friends had gathered at the colony. "Look at what just a few people can do to really make a difference."

Mr. Daniels, cuddling a fluffy tabby in his arms, added, "With some hard work and belief in what you're doing, well, anything can happen!"

Focus Questions   What obstacles does Maidie face? What must she do to overcome them?

The Claim

by Myra Smith

illustrated by Cheryl Kirk Noll

May 1, 1917

A cold spring wind greeted me as the neighbor's carriage brought me to the new claim. Mama always called this part of the Montana plains "such lonesome country." Perhaps that is why my parents sold their ranch when I was small. I remember quite a few things about the ranch—the horses, the wind, working in the garden. These are happy memories of when Mama was alive.

Our family's life has utterly changed since those days. We live in the busy town of White Sulfur Springs. For years, my job has been to keep house for my family of men, both young and old.

Now I am taking on a new challenge. "Maidie," Papa said one evening last month, "all the boys have taken on homestead claims. I am grateful because it helps our family build for the future. The Homestead Act states that a homesteader must be twenty-one years old to legally stake a claim on 320 acres of land. The law does not state whether that person should be a woman or a man. Women in Montana were given the right to vote three years ago. I say you have the right to a homestead like any other. Your brothers and I will help, of course. Do you care to try it, my dear?"

My heart leapt at the thought, and I immediately assented. What an adventure—and what an opportunity to contribute to my family's finances! And that is why I sit this evening in a small shanty built by my brothers. The woodstove crackles, and the kerosene lamp casts a soft glow across the modest room. Tomorrow I will survey this sizeable tract of land that is mine alone!

May 15, 1917

   My first diary entry is quite lengthy! Since that first night, I have not had a moment to reflect on life out here on the claim. From sunup to sundown there is always something new to do. The chores are never-ending! My brothers, Richard and Isaac, have helped me plow and seed a wheat crop. Neighbors pitched in, too, and we had the job done in three days. I am also fortunate to have a well for drinking water only a quarter-mile away. I have planted potatoes, carrots, and beans in a little garden. Each day I walk a new portion of the claim with my dog, Sal, by my side. The views of the Judith Mountains are beautiful, and the air is sweet. This is the life!

June 7, 1917

There has been just the right amount of sun and rain this spring, and I am starting to see the green flush of growing wheat spread across the fields. My claim is going to be a success; I can just feel it! If we can bring in an exceptional wheat crop this year, it will be a good start to gaining the legal right to this land. Tomorrow the "lads"—Richard, Isaac, George, and Papa—will come over for a celebration supper, for they sorely miss my cooking.

June 26, 1917

    My arms have grown so strong, what with lifting and hauling all day, that I hardly recognize myself when I look in the mirror. The wheat continues to thrive; it looks like the waves of a small ocean. The garden grows steadily. Yesterday I cut blocks of sod to stack along the outside of the shanty for keeping out the wind. Next year I will keep a few chickens and try planting flowers outside my door. I remember Mama loved growing chrysanthemums, snapdragons, and sunflowers.

July 15, 1917

    Disaster struck late yesterday afternoon when a dark cloud appeared in the distance. I thought it was a storm cloud, but it turned out to be a huge cloud of grasshoppers! They fell everywhere, like rain. They dropped on my beautiful crop and started chewing and chewing. Isaac rode up with the neighbor, and we did what we could, beating away the insects with empty seed sacks, but our efforts were useless. My beautiful crop is gone. I cannot write anymore tonight, for I am wholly heartbroken.

July 28, 1917
   The summer heat blazes, and the land looks barren and empty. There is no green at all. What will I do? Papa says perhaps I should come back into town and leave this land behind. "Maybe this was a bit too much for you to take on, my dear," he said. I know he means well, and perhaps he is right. When the sun sets and the air cools, Sal and I will take a walk so I can do some more thinking.

August 20, 1917
    I have decided to stay and try to farm my claim again next summer. I will tell Papa this evening. I have five years to make the crops succeed, and with the help of the family, I believe I can do it. I dearly love this land. I love the freedom and even the hard work. It is a joy to build something with your own hands. I feel like a fortunate young woman to have this chance. I cannot . . . no, I *will* not let this opportunity pass me by!

Focus Questions What drove Mary Kingsley to continue her travels in Africa? What important discoveries did she share with the world?

A Very Proper Hero

by Thaddeus Gibson

Born in the mid-1800s, young Mary Kingsley was considered a very "proper" English girl. Throughout her childhood, she did what most girls like her did. Schools were only for boys, so she learned to read at home. When her mother fell sick, Kingsley stayed home and took care of her. She gave up the idea of marrying.

When she was thirty, both her parents died. Like a dutiful sister, she moved in with her brother to take care of his household. But one day her "proper" life changed completely. Kingsley's brother left for a long visit to China. She was free at last to do what she wanted. She headed straight for Africa.

As a girl, Kingsley had read dozens of books on natural history. She loved learning about plants and animals. And she longed to visit places English people knew little about. So in 1892 she set off for what people called the "Dark Continent."

Though raised in ease and comfort, Kingsley chose the rugged life. She traveled by steamship to the African coast and then went up rivers by steamboat and canoe. And she always traveled alone—a feat considered very daring for a woman of her time. To pay for the trip, she became a trader. She brought along quantities of cloth, which she exchanged for rubber and ivory, a hard, white substance of which elephant tusks are made. Rubber and ivory were rare in England, so she could sell them at a good price.

While in Africa, Kingsley met many of the local people and also other traders. Soon she knew much about life there. Africans became used to seeing this slender young woman in a prim black dress, never without her umbrella.

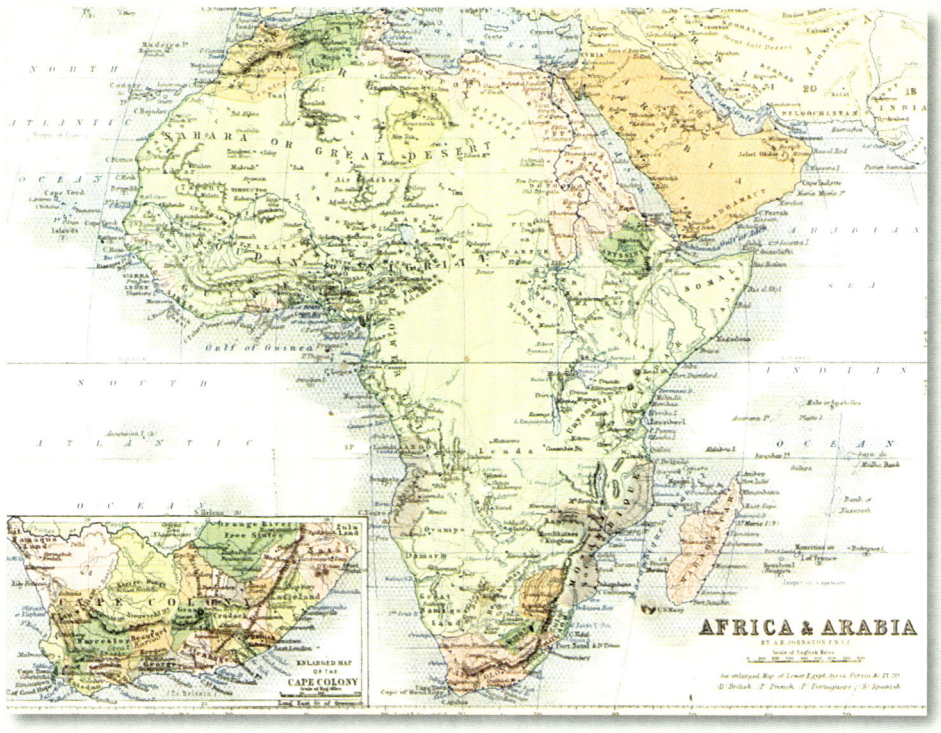

A map of Africa from the late nineteenth century

Kingsley enjoyed her time in Africa, but she did have some hair-raising adventures. One day, while walking through the jungle, she tumbled into a deep pit that was a trap set for animals. The bottom was lined with sharp spikes to stab the falling animal. Kingsley always wore several layers of skirts, as was the fashion in England. Luckily, the spikes could not get through them.

On another occasion, she was paddling a canoe along a stream when a hippo suddenly rose out of the water, its jaws gaping. Hippos do not like boats and can easily bite them in half. Kingsley could have attempted to flee, but she decided to make friends with the creature instead. As she wrote later, "I scratched him behind the ear with my umbrella, and we parted on good terms."

When Kingsley returned to London, she brought a little of Africa with her. A tiny pet monkey perched on her shoulder wherever she went.

Mount Cameroon

In 1894 Kingsley made a second African trip. This time the British Museum hired her to bring back plants, animals, shells, and other things of interest. She collected hundreds of items. Three kinds of fish she found had never before been seen by Europeans. Scientists named the fish for her. Kingsley also spent time living among a people known as the Fang, recording facts about their culture.

Nothing seemed to hold Kingsley back. One day she decided to climb Mount Cameroon, one of the highest volcanoes in Africa. She was the first European woman to do so. After reaching the top, she was caught in a tornado and nearly died. Not long after that, she came face-to-face with a gorilla. Few non-Africans had ever seen one before. In fact, many thought they were made-up creatures of local legend. She also had some close calls with crocodiles, snakes, and other wild animals.

At the conclusion of this journey, Kingsley wrote a book titled *Travels in West Africa*. It was a huge best seller. She became a highly popular speaker as well. People flocked to her speeches to listen and to see Africa in what was then a novel way—through a woman's eyes.

Encouraged by this success, Kingsley wrote a second book, *West African Studies*. In it, she voiced some ideas people were not used to hearing. She spoke respectfully of African peoples and argued against those who wanted to do away with African cultures or make them more like those of England. The book prompted heated disagreements. But her work was revolutionary. From then on, the British government seemed ready to have a higher regard for the people of Africa.

In 1899 Kingsley began a third trip. This time she went to South Africa, at the very tip of the continent. She had planned to collect more fish for the British Museum, but there was a war on. England was fighting a group of settlers called the Boers for control of an area where gold had been found.

Kingsley immediately went to the army and offered to serve as a nurse in one of its hospitals. Instead, the army sent her to care for Boer soldiers in a prison camp. Conditions there were terrible. The air was full of deadly germs, and before long Kingsley caught typhoid fever. She died on June 3, 1900, at the age of thirty-eight.

In her short life, this "proper" young woman had accomplished things no other person—female or male—of her time could have done. An explorer, naturalist, humanitarian, author, and faithful daughter and sister, Kingsley was a hero many times over.

Focus Questions What inspires Maya to make her films? How does she make her dream come true?

Maya's Dream

by Richard Shannon
illustrated by Carol Newsom

As a hush fell over the packed theater, Maya closed her eyes. She could feel small beads of sweat form on her forehead. Her category was next. The biggest names in the movie industry were seated around her, dressed in the finest suits and designer gowns. Maya felt out of place, yet she knew she deserved to be there.

She had started with nothing, but she had made it. Here she was, waiting for her name to be read from a list that included the best of the best. She closed her eyes and thought about the path she took to get here.

When she was growing up, both of Maya's parents worked long hours, but the family still struggled to pay the bills. When Maya was old enough, she got a job washing dishes at the local diner. Every week Maya handed her pay over to her mom with a smile. Her mother gave her a five-dollar bill to keep for herself. Maya hid the money in an old shoebox so her brother would not find it.

Maya's family lived in an apartment then. It had two bedrooms and was on the fourth floor of a five-story building called Fountain Court. The apartment was small and in desperate need of repair, but it was home.

Maya loved Fountain Court and all the kind neighbors who felt like family. Like her own family, which had emigrated from Puerto Rico, her neighbors were from many different countries. She often sat with her neighbor Mrs. Tavares, who spoke Portuguese to the birds she fed in the courtyard. The Bonillas, a couple who lived three doors down, had been married for nearly fifty years. They still danced in their living room to old waltzes. Maya loved to sit on their couch and watch them dance. She would watch everything as if it were a film being created before her eyes.

For her twelfth birthday, Maya went to a theater matinee. It was the first time she had seen a movie on the big screen. She loved every part of it: the lighting, the music, and the words. After that day, movies were all she could think about. But her school had no classes on acting or music. They had been cut a few years before because of a lack of funds.

So Maya spent as much free time as possible at the local library, borrowing movies and books about film. She would watch the movies on the old VCR in the living room and study them like homework.

  At fifteen, she used those hidden five-dollar bills to buy a used video camera and started filming the things she saw around her. Her home and her neighbors were a favorite subject. She watched what she filmed over and over, learning which sounds and images fit together and which did not. She planned film screenings for her family, friends, and neighbors. In their minds, Maya was a movie director already. But she knew she was not a professional yet; she needed to learn the art of making movies from an expert.

Maya's parents did not have money to send her to college, but she did not let this end her dream. Through hard work and determination, Maya earned a partial scholarship to attend a local college. With her job at the diner and a student loan, she was able to pay for the rest of the tuition.

During her college years, she made many films on many subjects. But she continued filming her friends and neighbors at Fountain Court. By the time she was twenty-five, Maya had ten years of film about Fountain Court. She had kept all of it!

It was Mrs. Tavares's death that was a turning point for Maya. She missed her old friend and began to watch her film footage of the charming woman to keep her close. One night Maya got an idea. Why not keep Mrs. Tavares alive through film? A documentary about her friend would make a wonderful tribute. She could include her other neighbors too. It took her five years to finish, but she did it. It was this documentary that had brought Maya to this awards ceremony.

The applause broke Maya's daydream. She had not realized it, but her name had been called. She had been chosen as the best of the best. She opened her eyes, wiped away the tears, and walked proudly to the stage. The award in the category of "Best Documentary Film" went to Maya Louise Delgado's *The Kings and Queens of Fountain Court*.

Unit 1

Focus Questions What does a butterfy represent to you? What does a cocoon make you think of?

Getting Ready to Win

by Sandra Liatsos
illustrated by Ken Tiessen

When I lose
    and I'm defeated,
feeling gloomy
    and depleted
I become a caterpillar
weave myself
    a silk cocoon
grow and dream
I've reached the moon . . .

Soon I feel
    my wings of power
growing stronger
    by the hour
till they rise
    to meet the light—
reaching high
    I shine in flight.

Hang In There

Poetry Reflections

These questions can help you think about the poem. Write your answers. Then talk about them with a partner.
- The speaker in this poem says he or she becomes a caterpillar when discouraged. What do you think the speaker means by this?
- At the end of the poem, the speaker rises "to meet the light" and says, "I shine in flight." What is happening to the speaker?
- This poem describes a way to face challenges and overcome obstacles. Do you have a way of doing this? Explain.

Reading Reflections

These questions can help you think about the stories you read. Write your answers. Then talk about them with a partner.

Focus on the Characters

- Alejandro is overwhelmed at first in "Wilderness Lessons." Hiking is much more difficult than he thought it would be. Why do you think he chooses not to give up?
- In "A Very Proper Hero," why do you think Kingsley was so respectful of African peoples?
- Maya makes a documentary to honor her neighbor, Mrs. Tavares, in "Maya's Dream." Who and what else does she honor in that documentary?

Focus on the Stories

- In "Making a Difference," six friends work hard to help two men and a group of cats. Tell how a character in another story works hard to help others.
- Powell sets a goal for himself in "John Wesley Powell: Brains and Grit." He decides to travel the Grand Canyon by boat. No one else had ever done that. Name another story with a character who is the first to do something.
- Some goals take a lot of physical work. Think about "The Claim" and "Wilderness Lessons." Compare and contrast Maidie and Alejandro's hard work.

Hang In There

Focus on the Theme

- Some of this unit's stories tell of people working hard to reach personal goals, while some tell of people working hard to help others. Which kind of work would be more challenging for you? Why?
- In "Wilderness Lessons" and "The Claim," the main characters have other people cheering them on. Why might that make it easier for them to hang in there?
- In your opinion, which character faced the most difficult challenge? Why?

Focus Questions Why is Nobu punished? Why is Ichiro more deserving of wealth?

To Celebrate the New Year

a Japanese folktale retold by Pamela Haskins
illustrated by Phyllis P. Cahill

A proper celebration of the new year, called Oshogatsu in Japan, is very important. It sets the stage for all that is to come in the following months. That is why a poor young man by the name of Ichiro Takahashi was so dismayed to find his cupboards empty of rice just one day before the new year.

Ichiro went to speak with his brother, Nobu, a wealthy landowner who was known for his greed rather than his generosity. "Have you any rice to spare?" asked Ichiro. He stared in disbelief at the bulging cupboards.

Tight-lipped, Nobu shook his head. "You'll have to make some other arrangement for your new year's rice."

As Ichiro began walking dejectedly toward home, he encountered a stooped old woman carrying a basket. "May I help you?" he inquired politely.

The old woman looked up with eyes as bright as a sparrow's. "How kind of you," she replied, handing him her basket.

When they reached her farmhouse, the old woman took a small wheat cake from her basket and handed it to Ichiro. "Take this with you into the woods," she instructed. "Look for a band of small men at the edge of the clearing. See whether they are willing to trade a mortar and pestle for your cake. Accept nothing in its place."

Ichiro felt the temperature drop as he entered the densely wooded area. He walked for a few minutes, enjoying the mossy stillness, before coming upon the clearing and the tiny people. A group of about twenty were building a small structure, while others practiced a dance nearby.

"Have you come to work or dance?" demanded one man.

"N-n-neither," stammered Ichiro, taken by surprise. "An old woman told me you might be interested in making a trade for my wheat cake."

"Of course," said the man. "I have some gold coins I'd be willing to trade." He hoisted a bag on his small shoulder and looked at Ichiro.

"I'm afraid that won't do," said Ichiro apologetically.

"Perhaps you'd prefer these jewels," said a dancer, holding up two sparkling stones.

"Thank you, but that's not what I had in mind."

"This mortar and pestle then," said the man, handing over a small marble bowl.

"That was the trade I had hoped for," said Ichiro. The tiny man demonstrated the special powers of the small bowl and the club-shaped mashing tool. Ichiro paid close attention. Finally he bowed in thanks and bade the group farewell.

When Ichiro arrived home, he was bursting with excitement.

"What does it do?" asked his wife, Kasumi.

"Rice, rice, we shall have plenty of rice!" exclaimed Ichiro, pulling the pestle gently to the right. Rice began pouring from the small bowl. Kasumi laughed with joy as she grabbed a bag to hold the grains.

When four bags had been filled, Ichiro ordered the bowl to stop and pulled the pestle to the left, just as he had been shown. "What else would you like for your new year's celebration, my dear?" asked Ichiro gleefully. "Some buckwheat soba noodles? Decorations for the front gate? A new house in which to celebrate?"

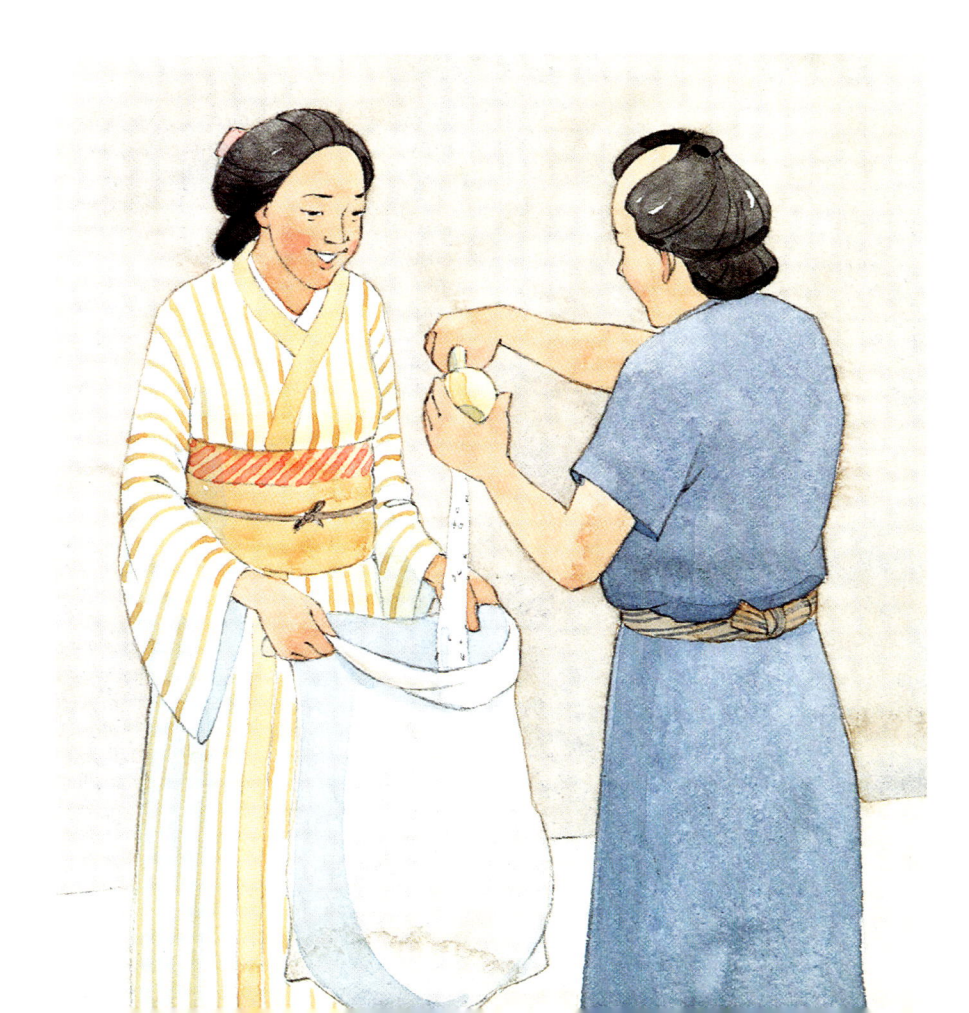

By early evening, a grand home stood in place of the Takahashis' humble shack. The cupboards were full of all the delicacies befitting a new year's celebration. The gate was decorated with a rope made from straw, fern leaves, and an orange for luck. When the guests began to arrive, they were amazed at how quickly the Takahashis' fortune had changed.

At the end of the evening, Ichiro used the mortar and pestle to make candies for all the children. He listened to the 108 chimes of the nearby temple bell and felt blessed for the good fortune that surrounded him.

Just as Ichiro was making the candies, Nobu walked by and noticed what his brother was doing. Nobu swallowed his jealousy and waited until later that evening when the house was finally quiet. He crept into the dark kitchen and pocketed the mortar and pestle. Then he stole into the night, gloating over his treasure.

When Nobu reached the ocean shore, he hurriedly untied the rope of his small boat. He climbed inside and began rowing toward the island where he lived. When he became hungry, he ate a bite of the rice cake in his pocket. It lacked flavor, though, and needed a bit of salt.

As he had seen his brother do, Nobu pulled the pestle to the right. He smiled as salt began flowing from the marble bowl. It poured into the boat. But then Nobu became alarmed, for he had no idea how to make it stop. He tried shaking the bowl and managed only to drop the pestle into the inky black ocean. The boat continued filling rapidly with salt and sank only minutes later, taking Nobu and the mortar to the bottom of the ocean with it.

Ichiro never did find out what happened to the mysterious mortar and pestle, nor to his brother. Nobu was never heard from again. To this day the mortar remains at the bottom of the sea, still filling the oceans with salt.

Focus Questions How is Arachne punished for her boastfulness? Why do you think the Greeks told this myth?

Arachne's Web

a Greek myth retold by Felipe Salgado
illustrated by Janet Nelson

Many, many years ago in the ancient kingdom of Lydia, there lived a young woman named Arachne. Arachne possessed many fine qualities. But what she was best known for was her superior skill at weaving. When she sat at the loom, her fingers flew at lightning speed. She created tapestries that were lovely to behold. The colors were rich, and the images looked as though they might come to life at any moment. Some people said Arachne must have been trained by Athena, the goddess of weaving.

Arachne scoffed at such talk. She believed her own weaving to be the greatest in the land—far better than Athena's. Now Arachne may have had many talents, but she was a foolish and boastful young woman. Was her weaving superior to Athena's? Perhaps. But few people were unwise enough to compare themselves to gods and goddesses. The consequences were sure to be severe.

Athena heard of Arachne's boastings and was angered. How dare a mortal compare herself to a goddess? In spite of her anger, however, Athena had a forgiving heart. She believed Arachne to be deserving of a chance to redeem herself.

On a bright spring day, an old woman paid a visit to the small, tidy home Arachne shared with her mother. She rapped on the door with the top of her cane and was invited inside by Arachne's mother. The woman had a small owl perched upon her shoulder.

Arachne sat at her loom. She showed little interest in the guest's arrival. "What lovely work," said the old woman, pointing to a finished tapestry.

"Yes," agreed Arachne, "it is the finest in the land. No one, not even Athena, can create such perfect weavings."

"Have you no concern for angering Athena with your comparisons?" the old woman inquired. She looked at the vain young woman sitting before her. "Is it not wiser to show the respect the deities are due?"

Arachne shook her chestnut curls. "If Athena cares to dispute my claim, I welcome a contest that would prove my talents."

Then the old woman, who was really Athena in disguise, transformed herself back into a goddess. She was determined to teach Arachne a lesson.

If Arachne was startled by the turn of events, she hid it well. Within minutes, Athena and Arachne began to work feverishly. The room was silent but for the steady whirring and clacking of the looms. Athena's owl perched nearby where he had a better view of her nimble fingers.

As the day wore on, Arachne's worried mother and the owl were not the only observers. The citizens of Lydia had heard rumors of the contest and the foolhardy girl who had challenged a goddess. They were clustered in groups around the small house, trying to glimpse the weavers.

Finally the tapestries were complete. Athena had chosen to weave an image of her contest with Poseidon for the city of Athens. From mere threads, she had created a scene that was beautiful and powerful.

Arachne depicted the great god Zeus in various scenes, but all of them were less than honorable. The observers were shocked that once again Arachne had shown such a lack of respect to the deities. Still, there was no denying she had held her own in the contest with Athena.

Arachne turned smugly to Athena. "Look all you wish, but my weaving is faultless as I had promised. Is it not?"

Athena was filled with rage at Arachne's disrespect and boastful nature. In moments she had destroyed both the tapestry and the loom that had created it. She turned to Arachne, ready to loose her anger on the young woman. She was stopped by the pleas of Arachne's mother, who begged Athena to spare her daughter's life.

Athena agreed, but she was unable to leave without punishing Arachne. By the time Athena and her owl had made their way through the crowd, something amazing was happening inside the house. Arachne's limbs were rapidly growing longer and thinner. Somehow there seemed to be more than just four of them. And each began to sprout coarse black hairs. Her head began shrinking in size. She could feel her body begin curving in on itself.

The citizens peered into the windows in shocked silence as the spider in the corner began weaving her web from the pile of colorful threads. There was little doubt as to who the winner of the contest was.

Focus Questions What are some of China's ancient stories? How can they be seen in Chinese culture today?

Chinese History, One Story at a Time

by Heather Vance

Through music, dance, and word of mouth, the Chinese have passed along some of the world's oldest and most colorful myths and legends. These stories link modern China with the traditions of the ancient past.

Some of these tales tell of Chinese heroes. The people in these legends are real, though their stories may be exaggerated. They often lived so long ago that it is hard to tell fact from fiction. But these heroes all gave something special to Chinese culture. When young children hear these stories, they learn about the value of hard work, good deeds, true love, and perseverance. These are all qualities that are admired in their society. In America, stories of Harriet Tubman and the Underground Railroad or George Washington and the cherry tree serve a similar purpose. These tales reflect American culture and values just as Chinese legends reveal the qualities admired in Chinese culture.

One Chinese legend may be familiar to you. It is the story of a brave young girl named Mulan who lived during the sixth century. When she was small, she learned about the art of war from her father. He taught her all he knew about how to fight and how to defend herself.

When Mulan was a teenager, the emperor called her father to war. He was old and sick, and Mulan knew he could not go. So she cut her hair, dressed as a boy, and went to war in her father's place. Of course, the brave young woman saved her father's life. But she also proved to be a strong and honorable warrior. Although Mulan lived and died hundreds of years ago, she is kept alive in legends. Similar tales tell of famous poets, artists, and ancient leaders who showed great loyalty or bravery.

Chinese philosophies, or ways of thinking, play a major role in another type of myth. These myths are a way to spread the teachings of Chinese culture. For example, the point of a Buddhist story might be that good deeds will be rewarded or that all living things deserve respect.

One popular tale teaches an important lesson of Confucius, who was a wise and respected philosopher. In the story, a boy named Min Ziqian loses his mother when he is quite young. His father's new wife does not treat Min Ziqian very well. He is often cold and hungry, while his two little stepbrothers are well cared for.

But Min Ziqian does not complain. Over time, his father learns of how his son is mistreated. Surprisingly, the boy defends his stepmother. When he grows up and his father dies, Min Ziqian even continues to support her. From this story, Chinese children learn to respect and obey their parents—one of Confucius's major lessons.

Like the myths of the Greeks or Native Americans, some Chinese myths tried to explain things in the natural world that science could not yet explain. One of the best known of these myths is the story of Pangu. Before the world was formed, a being named Pangu lived inside an egg for thousands of years. He finally grew so large that he broke the shell. The light parts of the egg drifted upward. The heavy parts floated downward. This created the sky and the earth. Pangu stood between the two to keep them separated.

   As he grew, so did the distance between the earth and the sky. Pangu finally died eighteen thousand years later. At this time, all the elements of Earth were formed from his body. His breath formed the wind and clouds. His eyes formed the sun and the moon. Pangu's blood became the rivers. His hair became the grass. No one knew for sure how the world was made, but this myth offered comfort because it explained the unknown.

Although science can explain many of these mysteries today, the stories are still very much a part of modern culture. Children learn them in school or on their grandparents' laps. Important mythical figures, such as dragons, are often carved into vases or other pieces of artwork. Operas and plays are based on characters from ancient stories. The same characters can even be found advertising products on Chinese television or entertaining children from the pages of comic books! There is no doubt these stories are survivors that will be alive for future generations to enjoy.

65

Focus Questions Why is the Tlingit woman taken to live with the frog people? Why is she sad at the end of the story?

The Frog Kingdom

a Native American Tlingit legend retold by Liza Cho
illustrated by Christy Hale

In a small Alaskan village, there lived a beautiful young woman whose father was the chief of the Tlingit people. Her hair was the shiny black of a raven's wing, and her eyes were the color of clouds brewing up a storm. The villagers had cooed over her from the time she was a tiny girl. It is no surprise that she grew up feeling rather superior about her appearance.

The young woman began to think about finding a husband. Her father had made several suggestions, but none seemed to appeal to her. She and her sister discussed her prospects one afternoon as they strolled along the edge of the lake. Soon they came across a small green frog. The sister stooped and picked it up, cupping it gently in her hands.

"How horrid," said the young woman. "Isn't it slimy? And look at those bulging eyes. I have no use for such creatures." She shuddered and took a step back.

The sister chuckled and shook her head. With one finger she stroked the frog's tiny backbone. She admired its coloring and long, delicate toes. Then she bent and let it hop back into the water.

The next afternoon, the young woman met just the man she had been hoping to find. He was tall and slender with smooth skin and large inquisitive eyes. He wore a beautifully beaded top that seemed to contain every shade of green found in nature. She agreed to marry him without hesitation. The young woman followed her new love to an underwater kingdom that lay hidden beneath the depths of the lake.

When she did not return home that evening, the woman's family became desperate with worry. They searched the village but were unable to find any sign of her. Just two days later, she was spotted sitting on some lily pads in the middle of the lake, surrounded by frog people. When the passersby tried to call to her, the frogs and the girl quickly disappeared into the water.

It was the sister who figured out what had happened. "We were walking by the lake several days ago when I stopped to look at a frog. She was repulsed by it and plainly said so. Perhaps the frog people have taken her away as punishment for her disrespect."

The young woman's family began to form a plan for her release. A feast was made, with contributions from nearly every member of the village. But when the food was presented to the frog people, they merely hopped back into the water, taking the chief's daughter with them.

Finally the chief decided to drain the lake. He could think of no other way to ensure his daughter's safe return. For several days the Tlingit people worked to pump the water into large trenches. Progress was slow, but they could see the level dropping bit by bit.

A strong marshy smell arose as they reached the muddy bottom. The musty scent filled the entire village. Instead of disturbing the people, though, the earthy odor only made them renew their efforts. It was not long before the chief's son was able to reach his sister and bring her home.

For several days the young woman rested in her bed. The mud had been carefully washed from her hair by her mother and her sister. The lake slowly refilled, and the musty scent no longer hung in every corner of the village. Finally she was ready to speak.

"I loved my husband and his people," she told her family in a voice that seemed lower and huskier than it had before. "I wouldn't have minded staying with them, if only I could have seen you, too, from time to time."

"We must be careful," she cautioned, "for the frog people understand our language. I was foolish," said the young woman as tears slowly dripped down her smooth cheeks. "I spoke without thinking, and with my words I hurt those who have been so good to me."

The chief gently dried his daughter's eyes. "We will make sure no one else makes the same mistake," he promised. "All our people will come to know your story. We will show the frog people the respect they are due."

Over time the young woman shared with the villagers the stories and songs she had learned in the frog kingdom. She adjusted to life on land again, but a touch of sadness was always in her eyes. She could often be seen sitting alone along the shores of the lake. She would stare out at the lily pads for hours at a time. The Tlingit people knew better than to ask her what she was thinking.

Focus Questions What are some tricksters from world legends and folktales? Which of today's popular characters are tricksters?

A World of Tricksters

by Marcos Mata

Spreading mischief and outsmarting others, the trickster figure is a common character in the stories of many cultures. Even if you have never heard of the trickster, you have probably come across this figure in folktales and fables or on television shows and in cartoons.

Tricksters are usually animals with human traits. Often they are underdogs. They use their clever wits to triumph over those who are bigger or more powerful. Tricksters may pull a prank just for the fun of putting one over on a fellow creature. Other times they use their skills to get what they need, one way or another.

One of the most famous trickster figures is Brer (or Brother) Rabbit. Many stories feature this sly character. Somehow he always manages to get the best of those around him. In East Africa, a common trickster is Hare. When the first Africans were brought to the United States, the tales of this tricky character came with them. In America, Hare grew into the beloved Brer Rabbit.

For the first African Americans, Brer Rabbit was an important symbol. He seemed small and powerless. This is how enslaved Africans often felt in their new country. In spite of appearances, though, Brer Rabbit could free himself from almost any trap. His cleverness gave him an advantage over those who seemed stronger.

It is easy to see how these tales inspired the first African Americans. As a bonus, they were often a good source of humor. Who would not smile at little Brer Rabbit outsmarting Brother Wolf in the garden they shared? And who would not find escape from everyday life while listening to a story of Brer Rabbit outwitting smug Brother Gator with his fiddle?

Another popular African trickster is Anansi the spider. Remember how Hare traveled across the ocean to become Brer Rabbit? In the same way, Anansi traveled from Africa to the West Indies. The Ashanti people tell the tale of how Anansi became the King of All Stories. To earn this title, the sky god tells the spider that he needs to complete some tasks. He must catch a jaguar, some hornets, and a fairy that cannot be seen. Through trickery and quick thinking, clever Anansi meets his goal. Like the Brer Rabbit stories, there are many tales of Anansi and his adventures.

In Native American legends, the trickster takes a different form. In tales from the Southwest and the Great Plains, Coyote plays the role. He has special powers and can change things from one form into another. Coyote is clever like Brer Rabbit and Anansi, but he does not always come out on top as they do. Sometimes his negative traits, like greed or jealousy, get him into trouble. In these stories, he is a cautionary figure, someone who warns listeners of the consequences of their actions.

In the Pacific Northwest, Raven is one of the most common tricksters. He is known for getting into all sorts of mischief. Sometimes Raven's plans backfire. Still, his adventures are also tales of survival.

In one story, Raven convinces his cousin, Crow, to host a feast. Raven tells Crow it will be the perfect place for all the animals to hear him sing. In his invitations, Raven makes it seem like he is the one who is holding the potlatch, or feast. Raven is wise indeed, for this means that he will be fed at other potlatches during the long cold winter. Raven has not done a speck of work. As always, though, his clever thinking supports his lazy habits.

It is not hard to find similar trickster figures all around the world. In South America, Fox is the well-known prankster of legends. Sometimes he is foolish like most of the other tricksters, but he is also a sly schemer. In Japan the fox is called Kitsune and can transform himself into other creatures and things. Reynard the Fox appears as a trickster in folktales from France and other European countries. No matter where you travel, you will find the trickster figure, wriggling his way out of sticky situations.

In today's world, tricksters can be found in many books and cartoons. Their antics never fail to amuse. The audience cannot wait to see how they will use their cunning and intelligence to get themselves out of trouble. Is it any wonder why tricksters have been popular in the stories of so many cultures?

Focus Questions What makes a good gift? Why is Binyamin's gift prized above the others?

The Sharing of Gifts

a Jewish folktale, based on "The Magic Pomegranate,"
retold by Avi Lublin
illustrated by Julie Downing

In a nondescript brick tenement house in the heart of Brooklyn lived Moishe and Rivka Blum and their three sons. One evening, after talking late into the night, the brothers devised a plan to see the world. They would each go their own way and see what adventures they might find in their travels. At the end of three years, they would meet again, each bearing an unusual gift from his journey.

Moishe would miss his sons terribly, but he let them go with an open heart. Rivka packed a satchel for each boy and stood upon her tiny balcony overlooking the busy street below. With tears in her eyes, she waved good-bye as her sons set out in different directions.

For the three young men, the following years passed in a blur. Yakov, the eldest, traveled far and wide, mostly on foot. In a San Francisco market, he happened upon a telescope. He used his shirttail to clean the dirt smudged on the lens, and then he looked through it.

He was amazed to see his mother bent over a washboard in the kitchen. When he turned slightly, he could see palm trees swaying on a tropical island. As he rotated further, he glimpsed a man climbing a snow-capped mountain and then a figure in flowing robes riding a camel.

"This, indeed, will make the perfect gift," he said confidently as he paid the vendor.

Asher, the middle son, had chosen to journey across the ocean. In a small store in Turkey, he came across a dusty rug. Its colors had faded, and it was nearly worn through in places. Still, something made Asher pick it up. He sneezed as years' worth of dust filled his nose, and the rug gave a twitch, seemingly on its own. Startled, he quickly let go, but the rug hovered in the air. "A flying carpet!" exclaimed Asher. "What better present!"

The youngest son, Binyamin, did not travel nearly so far as his brothers. Everything was so interesting that it was difficult for him to make it very far without stopping to watch a sunset or talk to a friendly child. When the three years had passed, he did not have many exciting adventures to share, but he felt fully satisfied by all he had seen.

As he started home, he passed an apple tree filled with fragrant blooms. Its single fruit was plump and red. "Just the gift," he thought admiringly, plucking the apple. Glancing back at the tree as he walked away, he was surprised to find no sign of it at all. "Hmm," he said aloud. "Perhaps this apple is more special than I had thought."

It so happened that the three brothers encountered one another as they walked down the familiar city streets only blocks from home. There was much exclaiming as they joyfully greeted one another. They continued to walk, eagerly sharing their stories and the gifts from their travels. As they peered through the telescope, each saw the same image: a beautiful young woman lying upon her bed, clearly very ill. Her parents stood above her, wringing their hands with worry.

"We must help!" exclaimed Yakov.

Within minutes, Asher's flying carpet had taken the brothers across the city to a section of town they had never before visited. The grand buildings sparkled in the sunlight, glinting as though they had been sprinkled with gold dust. In spite of their ragged appearance, the three young men presented themselves to the parents of the girl.

Perhaps out of desperation, the parents invited the brothers inside and allowed them to visit. Binyamin suddenly remembered the apple in his satchel. He swiftly sliced a sliver and fed it to the girl, whose name was Golda. She opened her eyes and smiled at him. As she gained strength, he fed her several more pieces. Everyone watched in amazement as she sat up and the color returned to her cheeks.

By this time, the brothers had begun to fall just a little in love with the beautiful young woman. Each hoped in his heart that she might see him as the man who had saved her life.

"Tell me," Golda said to Yakov, "has your telescope changed at all since it led you to me?"

Yakov glanced at the telescope that lay on his bag and shook his head.

"And has your magic carpet changed since it carried you here?" she inquired of Asher.

Asher regarded the rug folded in a neat square on the floor. "Not that I can see," he replied, shrugging his shoulders.

Golda turned and addressed Binyamin. "Your gift—did it change?" she asked.

"Well, yes," he said. "I fed most of it to you, so it is no longer whole."

Golda smiled, for there was no question in her mind which brother to choose. Binyamin had given the most of his gift, and in return Golda gave him her heart.

Focus Question What stories have you heard that feature dragons?

Dragon's Advantage

by Audrey B. Baird
illustrated by Tom Price

On a rainy day
over at the castle,

Dragon fearlessly
swims the moat

on his back,

giving no thought
to knights
in shining armor.

Knights, he knows,
never go out in the rain

for fear of rusting.

Legend Has It

Poetry Reflections

These questions can help you think about the poem. Write your answers. Then talk about them with a partner.
- Why would knights be afraid of rusting?
- The title of this poem is "Dragon's Advantage." What advantage does the dragon have?
- Knights and dragons are common characters in British legends. What are some other brave people and strange animals you have read about in the unit selections? What countries do these characters come from?

Unit 2

Reading Reflections

These questions can help you think about the stories you read. Write your answers. Then talk about them with a partner.

Focus on the Characters

- How does Arachne act toward Athena at the beginning of "Arachne's Web"? What lesson does she learn at the end of the story?
- A famous European fairy tale is "Cinderella," in which a fairy godmother helps Cinderella escape from her cruel stepmother and stepsisters. Compare and contrast Min Ziqian from "Chinese History, One Story at a Time" with Cinderella.
- How would you describe the character of Nobu in "To Celebrate the New Year"? Does he change at the end of the story? Explain your answer.

Focus on the Stories

- In "The Sharing of Gifts," the brothers rescue a sick girl from death. Tell about a character who is rescued in another story. Is this character glad like the sick girl? Why or why not?
- Tales often pass on traditions. Choose one story from "Chinese History, One Story at a Time" and one trickster tale from "A World of Tricksters." Compare and contrast the purpose of each story.
- Many old stories tell how something in the world came to be. Name a story in this unit that explains something in nature.

Legend Has It

Focus on the Theme

- In "The Frog Kingdom," the drained lake has a strange, musty smell. The smell is not explained. Many folktales contain elements that seem mysterious. Name another mysterious detail from a story in the unit. Explain what you think that detail means.
- Choose one tale from the unit. Explain the lesson it teaches. Do you agree with that lesson? Why or why not?
- Which character from the unit's stories is most like you? Why?

Focus Questions Why do we need the skeletal system? What are some interesting facts about bones?

The Skeleton—Top to Bottom

by Darius Jackson

The skeleton—comprised of dozens of different bones—has three vital jobs within the human body. The first is to protect the major organs: the brain, the heart, and the lungs. The second is to help us move, with support from our muscles. The third is to give the human body its shape. Without our bones, we would look like giant, formless jellyfish.

There are a number of interesting and sometimes surprising facts about bones in general. Most people have probably heard that an adult human has a total of 206 bones. A little-known fact, however, is that humans are born with more than 300 bones. As babies grow, some of their bones grow together to form one bone, thus reducing the overall bone count in the skeletal system. And here's another bit of bone trivia: the longest bone in the body is the thigh bone, or the femur, while the smallest bone is the stirrup bone in the ear, measuring about one-tenth of an inch. One final fact is difficult to believe but completely true. Humans and giraffes have the same number of bones in their necks! The giraffe's bones are, of course, much bigger.

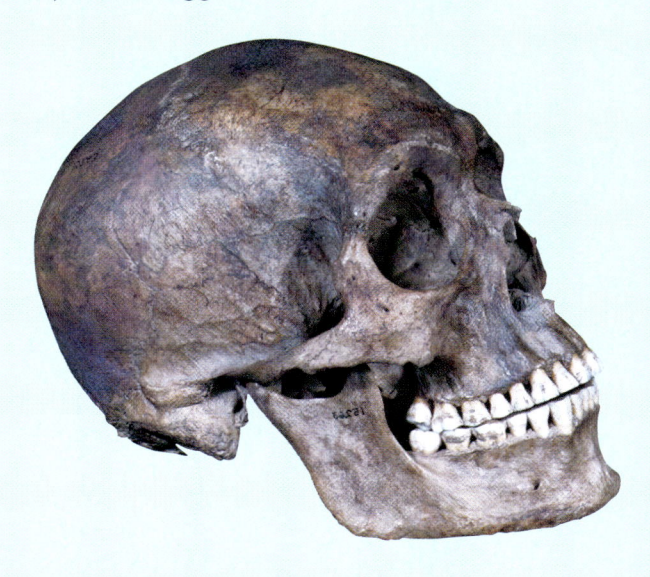

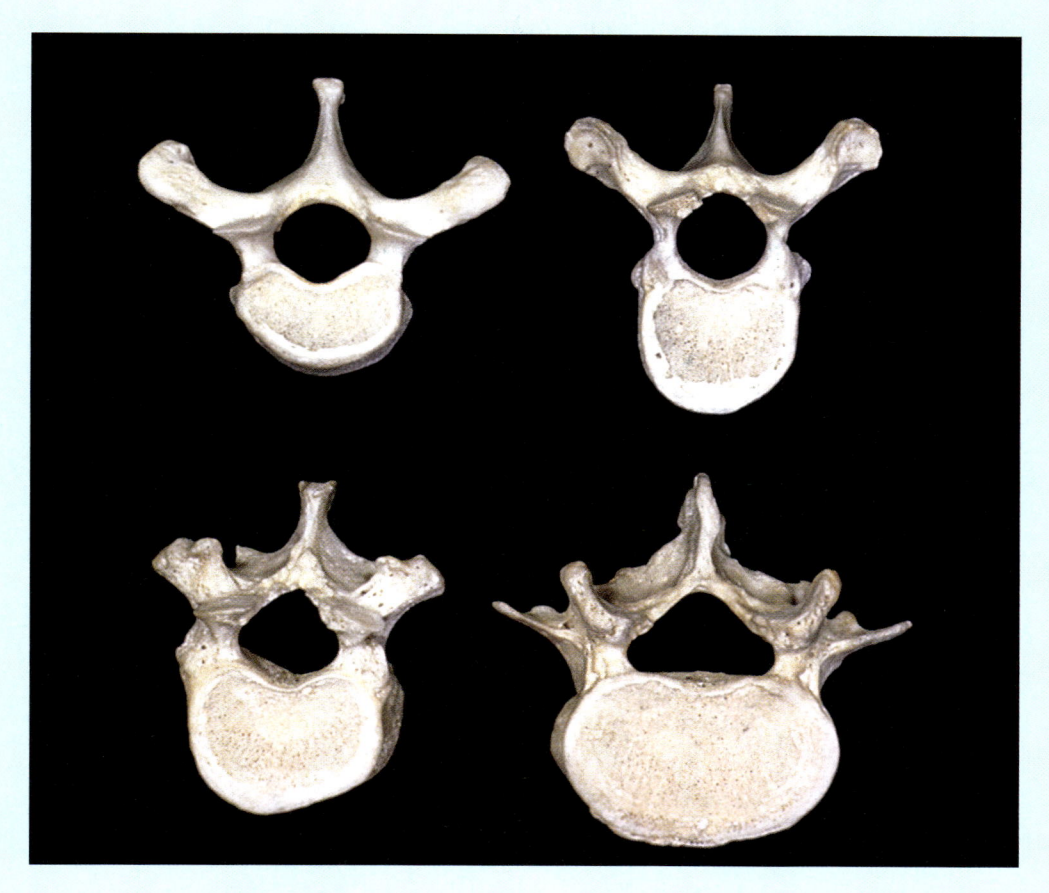

Human vertebrae

    The following survey of the skeletal system—from top to bottom—illustrates the role the bones play in the support and protection of the body. We begin at the top with the skull. The skull has two parts: the cranium and the facial bones. The facial bones support and shape the features of the face. The cranium has eight solid bones that are fused together to make a hard helmet of protection for the brain. The brain controls bodily functions, so it is important the human skull is tough and durable.

    The skull is held up by the twenty-six bones in the back called vertebrae. These small, round bones allow humans to stand straight. They also let us twist and bend. The vertebrae's most significant job, however, is to protect the spinal cord. This is the large rope of nerves that sends information from the brain to the rest of the body.

The vertebrae are attached to the ribs, the cage of bones inside the chest. Humans have twelve pairs of ribs that are divided between the left and right sides of the chest. The ribs have one of the biggest jobs in the whole body: protecting the heart and the lungs. Thanks to the ribs, these vital organs are able to circulate blood through the body and take in life-giving oxygen.

The bones of the arms are attached to the shoulder blades, or scapulae, and the collar bones, or clavicles. The arm is made up of three bones: the humerus, which is above the elbow, and the radius and the ulna, which are below the elbow. The eight smaller bones that make up the wrist are at the end of the ulna. The wrist bones lead to the bones that form the hand. The palm of the hand contains five separate bones called metacarpals. Each finger consists of three separate bones, while the thumb has only two.

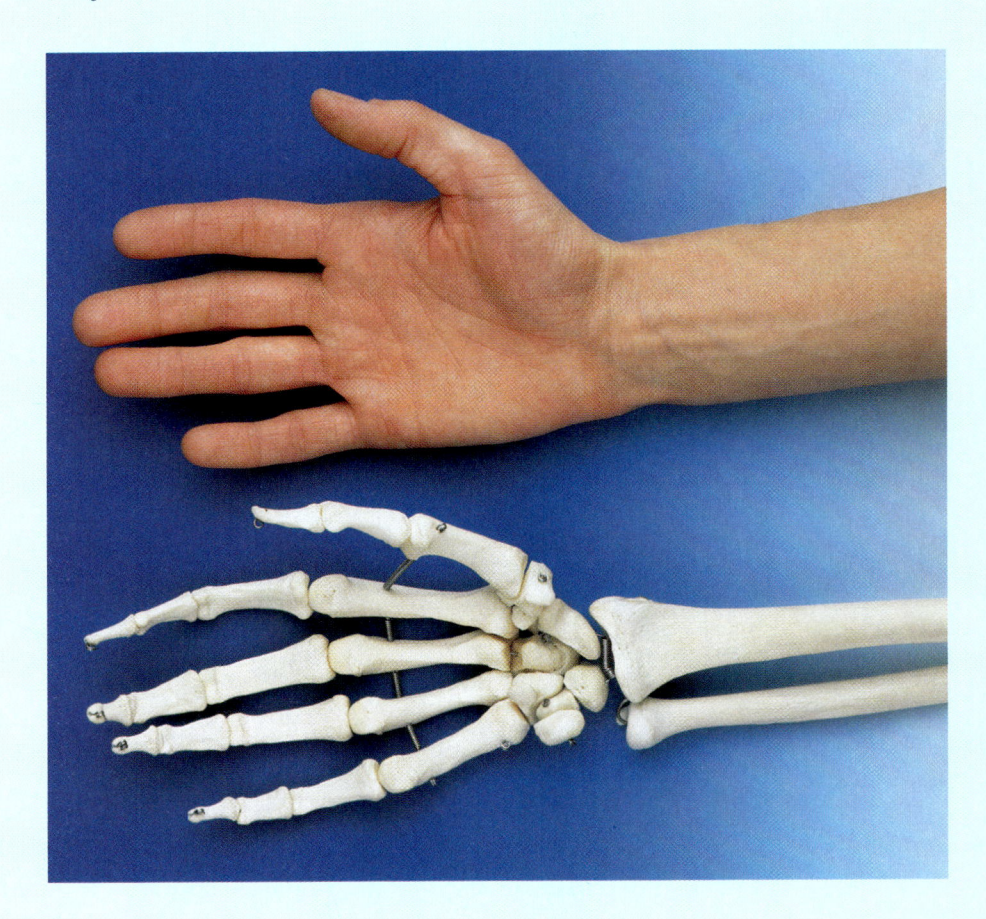

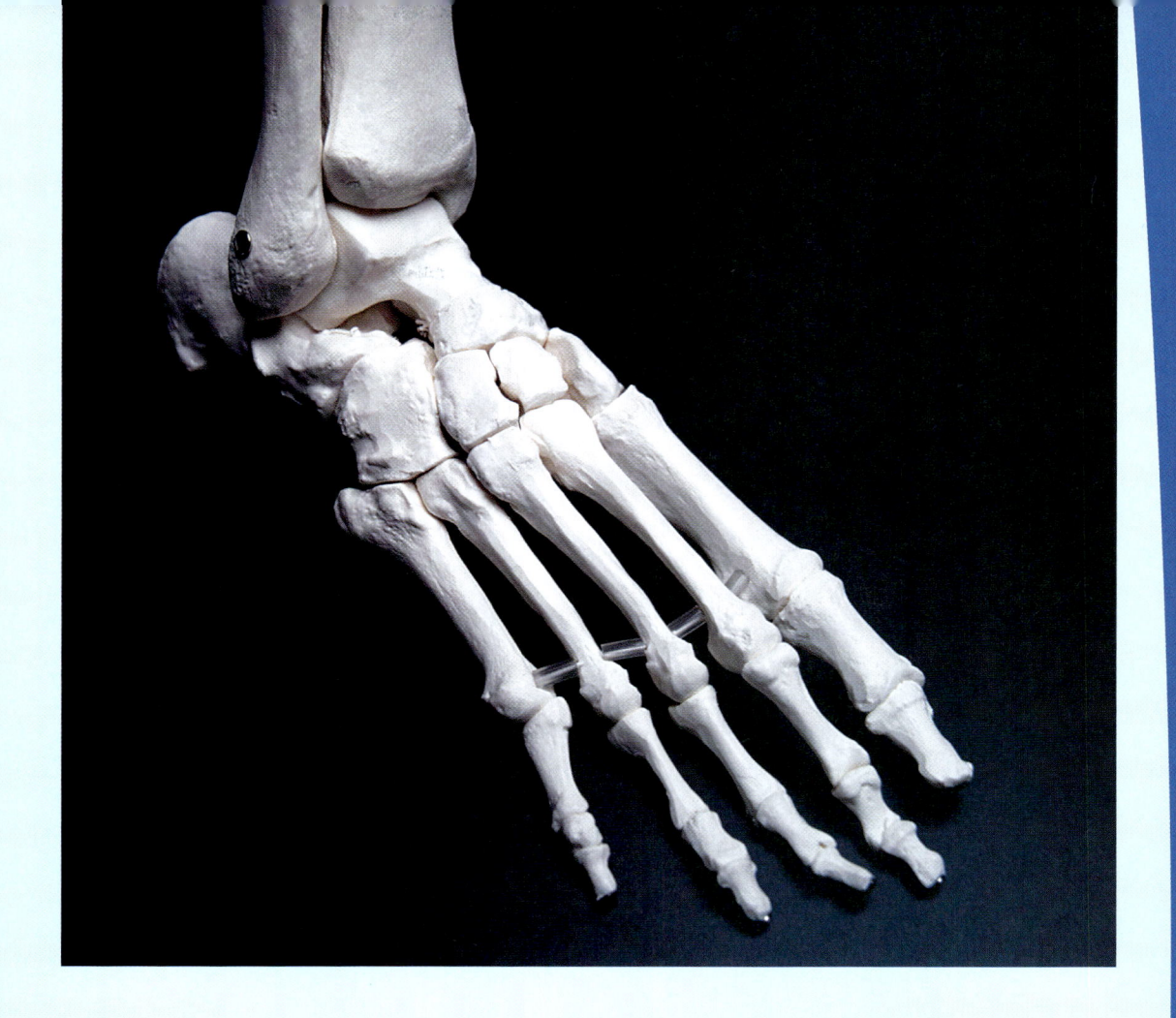

The long femur bone that makes up the upper leg extends from the pelvis, or hip, to the knee. The knee cap is a triangular-shaped bone that protects the knee joint. Below the knee are the tibia and the fibula. Together these strong leg bones support the weight of a human body. Finally, the bones of the ankles and feet are quite similar to those of the wrists and fingers. Five bones make up the main part of the foot, and each toe contains three little bones. Like the thumb, the big toe has only two bones. The bones of the feet are flat and wide and work together to help with standing and balance.

It is easy to see from their descriptions how the bones support our bodies and keep our organs safe. But how do the bones help us move? Bones move because of the joints, or spaces where the bones connect, and the muscles that are attached to the bones. When muscles contract and relax, they cause the bones, and us, to move.

We can see and feel the skeletal muscles that move our bones. When people work out or lift weights, these muscles become bigger and stronger, especially in the shoulders, arms, and legs. Skeletal muscles come in pairs. One muscle moves the bone in one direction, and another moves it back the other way.

The joints work closely with the muscles to produce movement as well. Joints provide flexible connections between the bones that allow the body to bend and twist in many different ways. Because of joints, the knees and fingers move back and forth like a door hinge. The shoulders and hips can move in a circular motion. However, the joints among the vertebrae allow only for slight movement.

That is the story of the skeletal system—from head to toe. To stand, sit, leap, skip, run, bow, and twirl, we need our 206 bones—and we need them to be healthy. A daily dose of calcium from dairy products will keep our bones strong and keep us on the go.

Focus Questions Why is Janet's presentation so challenging? Does she prove that she knows a lot about the ear and hearing?

Can You Hear Me?

by Elizabeth Watson
illustrated by Geoff Smith

"Alright, next we have Janet Robinson with her project on the human ear," announced Ms. Cardona.

That was my cue. I took a deep breath and willed my heart to stop thumping so vigorously. I was honored to be in my school auditorium that morning along with the other finalists in the annual science fair. I had prepared well for my presentation; I had memorized every word in my report and arranged my pictures, charts, and models to make an attractive display on the stage.

But there was one very big problem. The sound system was acting up again, and I would have to speak to the panel of judges without a microphone. *What horrible luck*, I thought as I mounted the stairs to the stage. *Everyone knows my voice doesn't carry. It escapes my lips and disappears as soon as it hits the air. I have enough trouble just being heard in class!* I needed an extra boost, so I decided to begin my presentation with a bit of fun.

I waited a few seconds after I got to the podium, collecting my thoughts. Then I looked up, flashed the panel a brilliant smile, and started my speech. "Elephants flap them, dogs perk them up, and people wiggle them. Even birds have them hiding underneath their feathers. Your ears allow you to hear all kinds of sounds, from quiet whispers to booming jet engines. But how much do you really know about ears and how they work?"

I stole a look at the judges and was surprised to see they were leaning forward in their seats and craning their necks toward me. They had strange looks on their faces, as if they were thinking hard about what I had just said. Some smiled slightly. *They must really be fascinated by the human ear,* I thought. I continued with my report.

"The human ear has three main parts: the outer ear, the middle ear, and the inner ear. Each part has its own job to do, and together they help you hear sounds," I said. I glanced at Ms. Cardona. She looked as if she had something to say to me, but I continued.

"To best understand how the ear works, it helps to understand how sound travels through the air in waves. If you've ever thrown a stone into a lake, you've seen the ripples moving outward, away from the source. Sound waves are similar. When someone speaks or plays an instrument, or when any sound is created, invisible sound waves travel out from the source of the sound. In order for sounds to be heard, these sound waves must be turned into actual sounds by your brain. Having two ears helps us detect the direction a sound is coming from. Your brain can tell in an instant whether the sound hit your right ear or left ear first. You can also quickly recognize the unique sound of a flute, a piano, or your alarm clock."

Suddenly Ms. Cardona interrupted me. "I'm so sorry to cut in, Janet. But we are having some trouble hearing you." The judges nodded in agreement. "Could you try to speak louder? Your sound waves aren't quite hitting our ears."

Everyone laughed at Ms. Cardona's little joke, and I tried to stop the blush that was slowly rising from my neck to my forehead. I took a very deep breath and forced the words out from deep in my chest.

"The outer part of the ear is called the pinna," I bellowed. "It's the part of the ear that's attached to your head. Much of the pinna is made from a flexible material called cartilage. The pinna's main job is to collect sounds. Think of it as a funnel that guides sound toward its center."

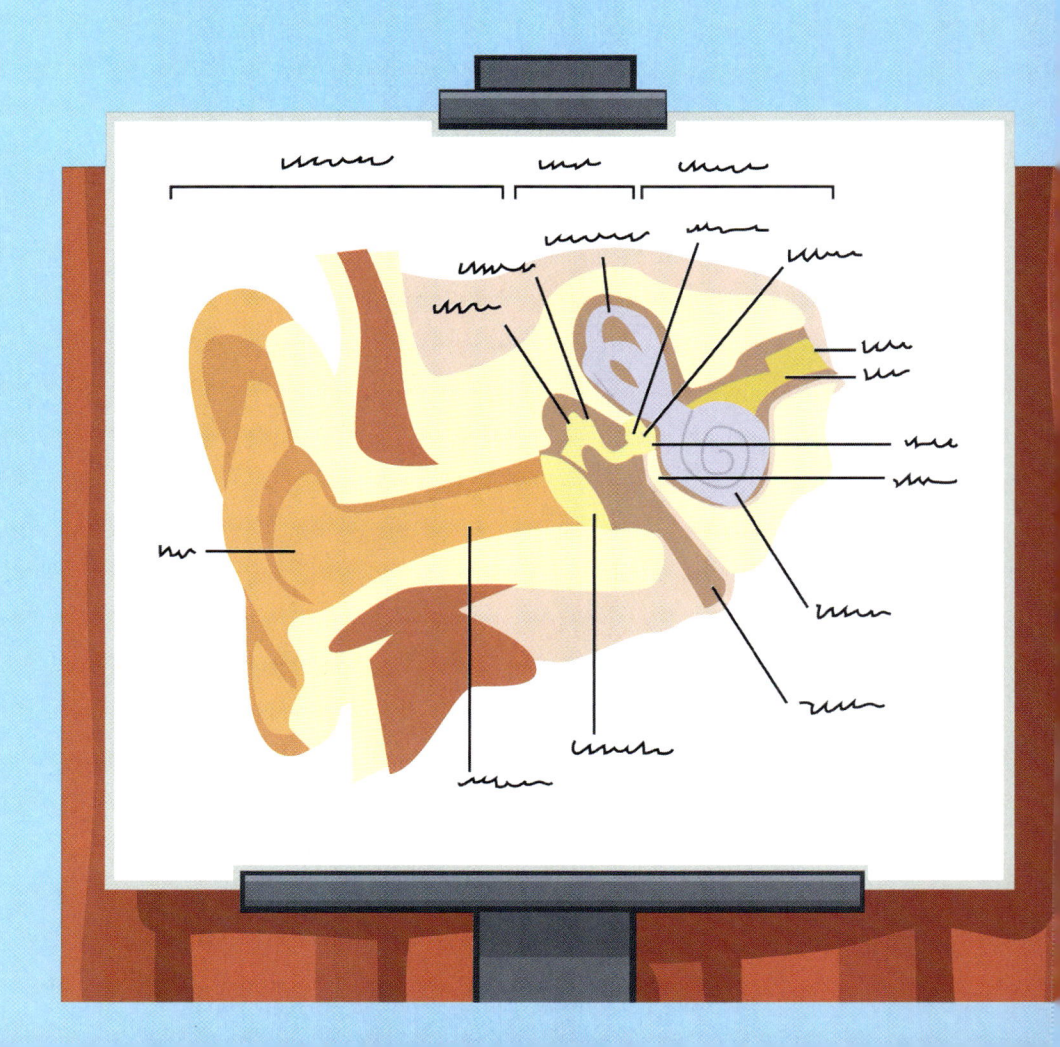

I paused. "Can you all hear me now?" I asked. I felt like I was shouting.

My audience nodded enthusiastically, and I continued. "Another part of the outer ear is the ear canal, which is the hole in your ear that you can see. As the sound waves move through the ear canal, they approach what's called the middle ear. The eardrum lies in between the outer ear and middle ear. The eardrum is a thin layer of tightly stretched skin, similar to the top of a snare drum.

"When sound waves hit the eardrum, it vibrates, and the waves are passed along to three tiny bones. These are called the ossicles, and they're the smallest bones in your body! They have interesting names that are based on their shapes. They're called the hammer, anvil, and stirrup. Sound waves go from the eardrum to the hammer first and make it vibrate. Then the hammer pushes the next bone, the anvil, which in turn pushes the stirrup. Finally, the stirrup pushes on a membrane that leads to the inner ear."

My voice was becoming hoarse, but I had to keep going. I explained to the judges how the sound waves then travel into the inner ear and hit a curled tube called the cochlea that is filled with liquid. The cochlea is lined with microscopic hairs. When the vibrations from the ossicles hit these hairs, they set the hairs in motion. This movement is a signal that goes to the nerve cells, which then send the message to the brain. Finally, the brain interprets the nerves' signals as a sound.

At last I was nearing the end of my presentation. I took a few more minutes to scream some facts about the inner ear and how it also helps us keep our balance. I think it is amazing how the semicircular canals do this. When we move our heads, the liquid in these canals stimulates tiny hairs that signal our positions to the brain. Then the brain knows what information to give our bodies to keep our balance.

After showing off my posters and the little model of the human ear I made, I could finally go back to my seat and give my voice a rest. It felt wonderful to be able to sit quietly and listen to the rest of the presentations. I tried not to be mad when I noticed none of the other students seemed to have trouble being heard.

I forgot my hurt feelings, however, when Ms. Cardona announced I had won first place in the science fair! "Congratulations, Janet," she said warmly. "Once we could hear you, I thought you gave us a very thorough explanation of how we could hear you." Everyone chuckled again at my teacher's wordplay. I just clutched my first-place trophy and made plans to drink some hot, throat-soothing tea when I got home.

Focus Questions How do smells trigger memories? What would your life be like without your sense of smell?

What's That Smell?

by Carlota Diaz

Think about your favorite smells. Do you recall the rich, sweet aroma of baking brownies? How about the sharp smell of freshly cut grass or the smoky smell of a campfire? Now think of unpleasant smells—those of stinky laundry or a misbehaving skunk. No matter what smell you are smelling, it adds significantly to your experience of the world. That smell may even trigger a distant memory. But how exactly do we smell in the first place?

The first part of smelling is as plain as the nose on your face. Smells come to you as you breathe through your nostrils, the two openings on the outside of your nose. The nostrils are separated by a thin wall called the septum. The septum is made up of cartilage, a tough, flexible tissue. If you push on the tip of your nose, you can feel how easily it bends. Your septum extends deep inside your nose. Close to your skull, your septum becomes a little tougher because it is made of thin pieces of bone.

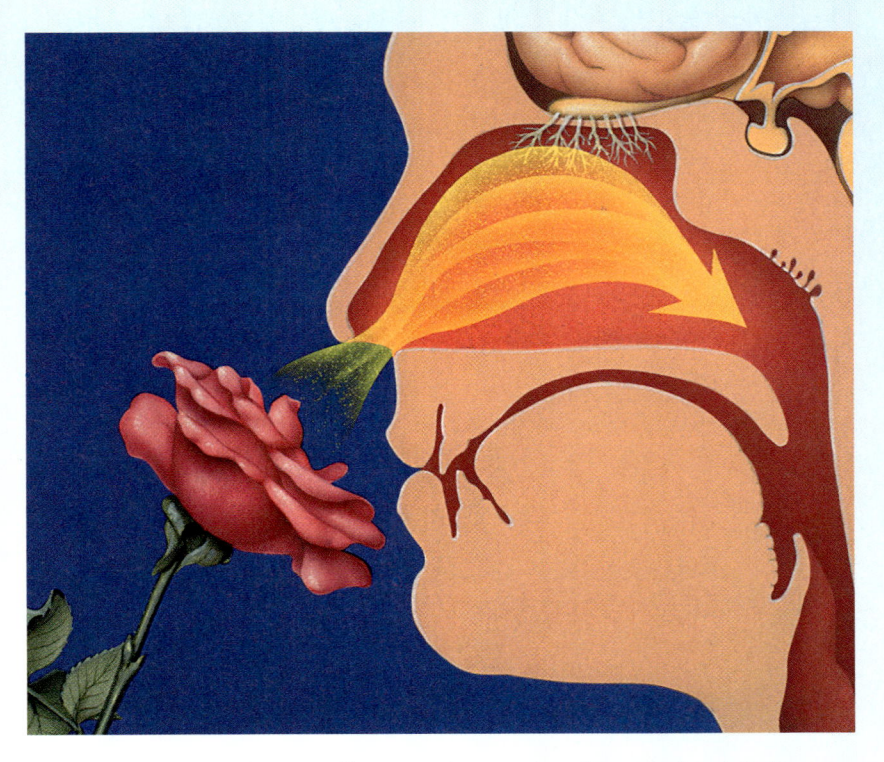

This drawing shows how smells enter the nasal cavity and stimulate the smell receptors.

   The nasal cavity is a large space found behind your nose. It connects with the back of the throat. The roof of your mouth, or palate, separates your nasal cavity from the inside of your mouth. The nasal cavity warms and cleans the air you breathe.
   When you breathe in, the air passes through your nostrils and into your nasal cavity before traveling down your throat into your lungs. If your lungs—and you—are to stay healthy, it is important that the air that enters your body is clean. To make this possible, the inside of your nose is lined with a moist, thin layer of tissue called a mucous membrane. The mucous membrane collects dust, dirt, and germs from the air you take in. Then when you sneeze or blow your nose, these unhealthful particles leave your body.

The mucous membrane has many little coworkers to help it do its job. These are the tiny hairs that run from the opening of your nose to the very back part of the nasal cavity. These tiny hairs, called cilia, move back and forth to push dirt and germs away from the back of your nose. Most importantly, they aid in the prevention of ailments such as colds and flu. But they also make a clear path for you to smell those brownies and that fresh-cut grass. You know how hard it is to pick up a scent when you are plagued with a stuffy nose!

Now here is where your sense of smell gets serious. The olfactory epithelium, at the top of the nasal cavity, contains tiny smell receptors that are sensitive to odor molecules in the air. You have millions of these receptors in your nose right now! When smells enter your nose, your smell receptors are stimulated. The smell receptors send signals along the olfactory nerve to the olfactory bulb. The olfactory bulb is just above the nasal cavity, underneath the front of your brain. The olfactory bulb sends these signals to the brain. The brain then turns these signals into smells you can identify.

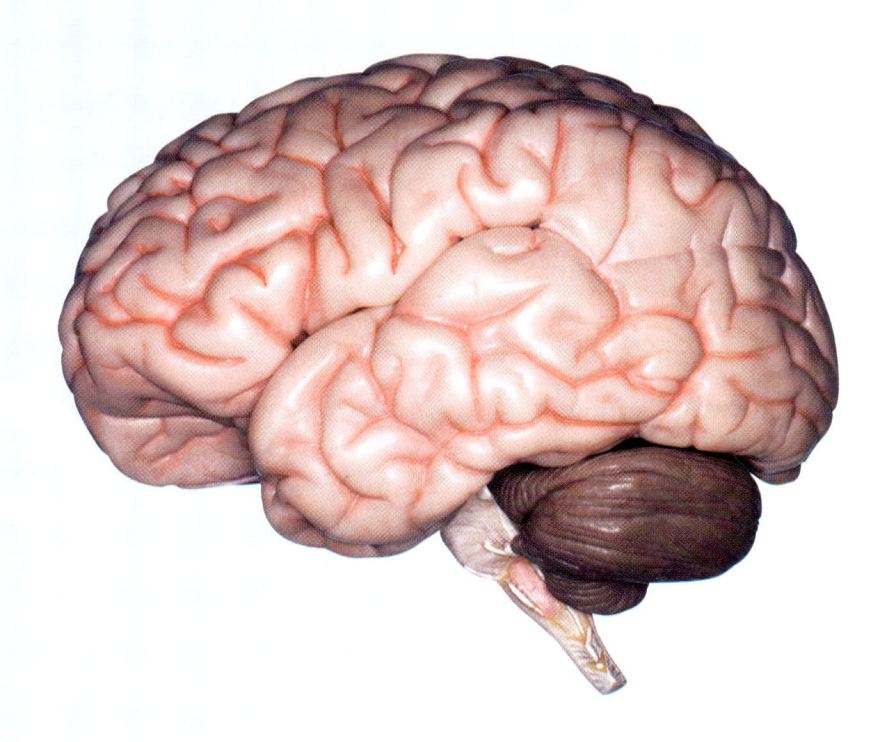

Your ability to smell has an important purpose besides treating you to a pleasing—or a revolting—sensory experience. It can help protect you from dangers in your environment. If you smelled smoke in your home, you would know something is wrong. Your brain would tell you there is likely a fire, and you would then go to a safe place. Your sense of smell also stops you from drinking sour milk or eating rotten food.

Furthermore, did you know your sense of smell also helps you taste? Think about it. Can you taste all that chicken soup you are eating when you have a respiratory infection? Probably not. When you have a clogged nose, the odors from that salty broth cannot travel to the receptors of your olfactory epithelium. Even though your taste buds are in fine working order, you still cannot taste a thing. This is because odors work with taste to help you fully enjoy your food.

Here is one final thing to remember: smells help us remember! The part of your brain that receives the smell signals from your olfactory bulb is closely associated with the part of the brain involved with emotions and memories. So one sniff of a particular odor can instantly cause your brain to recall a memory you have linked to that odor. Does the aroma of a certain food remind you of a family member who used to cook it for you? Does the smell of crayons and erasers make you think back to your first day of kindergarten? Then you have experienced firsthand the connection between smell and memory.

Your sense of smell is a powerful thing. It can save you from a host of dangers or stimulate your oldest recollections. And it can help you *really* enjoy that pepperoni pizza. Your nose knows the ability to smell is one of your most valuable senses.

Focus Questions Why was it so difficult for Elizabeth Blackwell to become a doctor? What inspired her to do so in the first place?

Graduation Day

by Judith Chen
illustrated by Marcy Ramsey

The church in Geneva, New York, was filled to the brim that January day in 1849. Ladies and gentlemen young and old had packed the majestic building with the columned porch, hoping to catch a glimpse of history in the making. The students of Geneva Medical College were graduating. But that was not what had caused such a stir. Soon a very special graduate would be making her appearance. Her name was Elizabeth Blackwell, and that day she would become the first woman in the United States to earn a medical degree.

As Blackwell and her brother Henry entered the church and strolled to their seats, they could hear the buzz of the crowd and feel the intense stares of hundreds of eyes on their backs. Blackwell surveyed the curious crowd with her usual dignity. She was proud, no doubt, of all she had accomplished. Her journey to this point had been a difficult one that daily had brought her face-to-face with opposition and prejudice.

Blackwell had not always thought she would be a doctor, but she was raised in a family that valued education—for boys *and* girls. This attitude was extremely rare in the early nineteenth century. Blackwell was therefore fortunate to have private tutors who taught her the same lessons they taught her brothers. With a firm knowledge of science and nature already begun, Blackwell moved with her family from her birthplace in England to America in 1832. The Blackwells lived in New York, then New Jersey, and then Ohio. When the death of Blackwell's father in 1838 left the family near poverty, Blackwell and her sisters had to become teachers to support themselves.

But teaching was not a fulfilling job for Blackwell. Surely there was something, she thought, that would allow her to use her mind and her abundant energy differently. Studying the organs and tissues of the human body was not the first goal she considered. An encounter with a sick friend, however, put the thought into Blackwell's mind in a hurry. The friend was enduring a long illness, and Blackwell visited her often. The friend told her she would have liked a female doctor to care for her. She also said Blackwell would be an ideal physician.

The idea grew in Blackwell's mind. There would be many obstacles. Women simply were not admitted to medical schools in her time. And she had no money to pursue her studies. But Blackwell continued to teach to earn tuition funds. She lived for a year in a doctor's house where she received medical training and studied books about the systems and functions of the human body.

When Blackwell began applying to medical schools, she knew her acceptance was unlikely. Dr. Joseph Warrington, a family friend, agreed. "Elizabeth," he said, "it is of no use trying. Thee cannot gain admission to these schools." The scores of rejections she duly received were not a surprise. Nevertheless, Blackwell knew she had to keep trying. She was smart and hardworking enough to become a doctor. Certainly someone would eventually see this. Her day of triumph came when a letter arrived from Geneva Medical College in the state of New York. She had been admitted after a vote by the students. The students had voted in her favor only because they thought it was a practical joke. But that did not matter. She had been accepted. And when she arrived on campus in November of 1847, no one told her to go home.

Blackwell's next struggle was for the respect of her teachers and classmates. Her fellow students were friendly enough at first, but most disapproved of having a woman in their classes. Blackwell was even barred from attending some anatomy classes because it was deemed inappropriate for a woman to learn about the human body.

The people of the town of Geneva were even more unwelcoming. Many stopped to stare at Blackwell as she walked down the street—or even as she sat in her classes. Women of the town shunned her. Some called her insane. She often felt like a curious animal on display at a zoo.

The earnest, diligent Blackwell did win over her classmates—and the Geneva townspeople—in time. And when the day came for her graduation, she had the highest grades in her class. She had not only survived; she had been the best.

Now the president of the college, Dr. Hale, was presenting the diplomas. He called the students up four at a time, spoke to them in Latin, took off his hat, and handed them the very important documents. He called Blackwell last and by herself. She took her diploma and bowed. She turned to go back to her seat, but then she stopped and faced Dr. Hale again. "Sir, I thank you," she said. "It shall be the effort of my life to shed honor upon your diploma."

Applause filled the room as Blackwell took her seat. It was hard to tell where she would go from here. There would be more struggles ahead as she asked the world to accept a female doctor. But Blackwell was determined. She would use her skills to help others—especially women and children—live healthy lives. She would carry on so that others could too.

Focus Questions How does the eye work? Why do people sometimes need corrective lenses?

More Than Meets the Eye

by Sunrise Jones

Most people rely on their eyes more than any other sensory organ. In fact, of all the senses, sight stimulates the brain to carry out the most tasks. The brain processes many things related to vision, such as movement, shape, color, and distance. The eyes can focus on a tiny piece of lint on a shirt or on an airplane thousands of feet in the sky. Keep reading to find out how the eyes work and enable you to . . . keep on reading!

When you take a look at your eye in the mirror, you are seeing only the front portion. The eyeball is actually a full sphere that is fitted into a hollowed-out area in the skull called the orbit, or eye socket. Can you feel where your orbit begins up above your cheekbones?

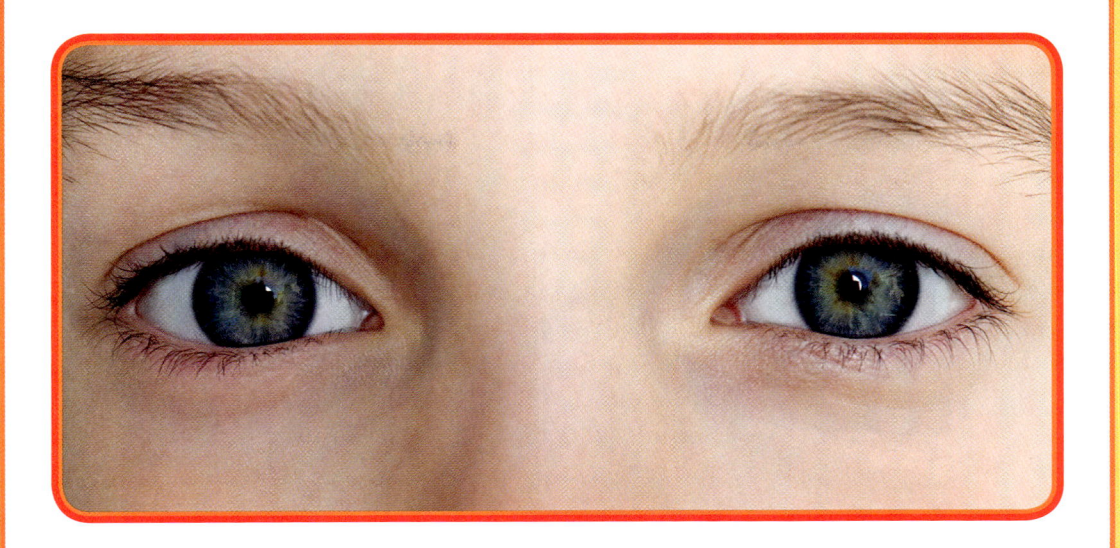

The white part of the eye is called the sclera. Blood vessels carry blood throughout the eyes, and sometimes you can see them as tiny red lines in the sclera. The colored part of the eye is called the iris. The iris can be blue, brown, green, or hazel, depending on the genes you have inherited from your family. But the iris does more than make your face distinctive. This colorful ring is made up of several muscles that open and close to allow light to enter the eye.

That light comes in through the pupil—the dark, round spot in the center of the eye. When it is dark and not a lot of light is available, the pupil is opened very wide to let in as much light as possible. The opposite is true when your eyes are exposed to very bright light. On a sunny day, the pupil closes tightly, making only a small opening for light to enter. Try looking in the mirror and experimenting with a small flashlight. You will see for yourself how the pupil opens and closes.

The transparent shield covering the front of the eye is called the cornea. Light travels easily through the cornea as it helps the eye focus. Each eye also has a tear gland behind the upper eyelid where tears are made. There is also a tear duct in the corner near the nose where tears drain away. It may surprise you to learn that tears do not just appear when you are crying! Every time you blink (which is every couple of seconds) tears wash your eyes. Tears prevent the eyes from drying out and help keep them clean and free from germs. Eyelashes and eyelids also help protect the eyes by keeping out dust and extreme light.

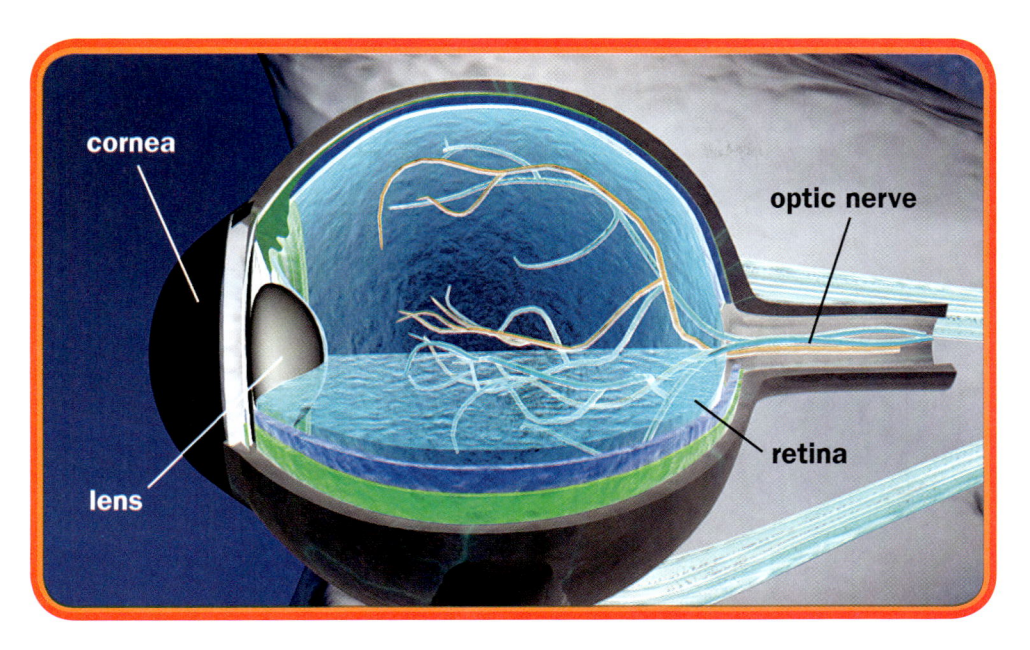

A view of the inner eye

    The process of seeing begins in this way. When you look at an object, light bounces off the object and enters the eye through the pupil. The light then passes through the lens. The lens works much like a camera lens to focus the light onto a membrane in the back of the eye called the retina. The result is that an image of what you are seeing appears on the retina—upside down! The retina has millions of light-detecting nerve cells called cones and rods. The cones help you see when light is bright and colorful. The rods work when the light is dull and dim. Millions of rods and cones make the retina very sensitive to light.
    The rods and cones change the light into electrical impulses that are sent through the optic nerve to the brain. The brain receives the signals and transforms them into a picture that you see. Of course, the image the brain has received from the retina is upside down. Luckily, the brain automatically knows to turn that image right side up.

Now that you know the basic process of seeing for one eye, you might wonder something. If humans have two eyes at slightly different positions, then those eyes are seeing slightly different things. Why then do we see only one image? It is true that each eye perceives something a little different. But once again the brain knows how to adjust to this situation. Because the two halves of the brain are connected, the brain can combine the images from both eyes to create one. It is like looking through a pair of binoculars. There are two lenses, but the binoculars form one picture.

You might also wonder about people who have impaired vision and wear glasses or contacts. Why does this process of vision not work for them? When someone needs glasses, it's often because the image that is supposed to be focused on the retina is not in the correct place. It might be just in front of or behind the retina. Glasses or contacts can then act as lenses to focus the image back on the retina and help a person see more clearly.

So now you see . . . there is a lot more to the eye than meets the eye!

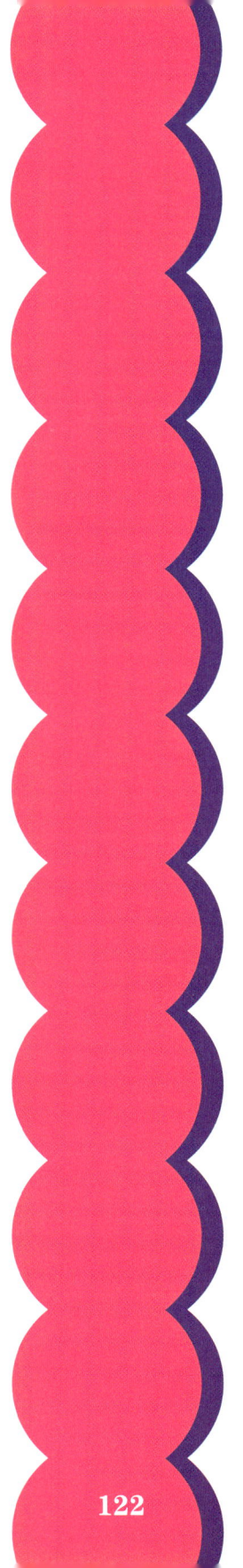

Focus Questions What are the main parts of the digestive system? How does food turn into fuel?

From Food to Fuel

by Vivek Kumar

You need energy to work, play, breathe, and even to read this sentence. Just like a car, your body must take in fuel and convert it to energy so it can perform all its functions. That is where the digestive system comes in. The digestive system takes in fuel in the form of food, breaks it down, and sends it all around the body to be used as energy.

Sometimes when people think of digestion, they think only of the stomach. The stomach *is* one part of the system. But there are many parts and many steps to the digestion process. Digestion starts with your teeth and your mouth. As you chew food, the moisture in your mouth called saliva immediately begins to break down the cellular walls of the food. The saliva comes from special glands inside the head near the ear, tongue, and jaw, called salivary glands.

tongue

epiglottis
esophagus
windpipe

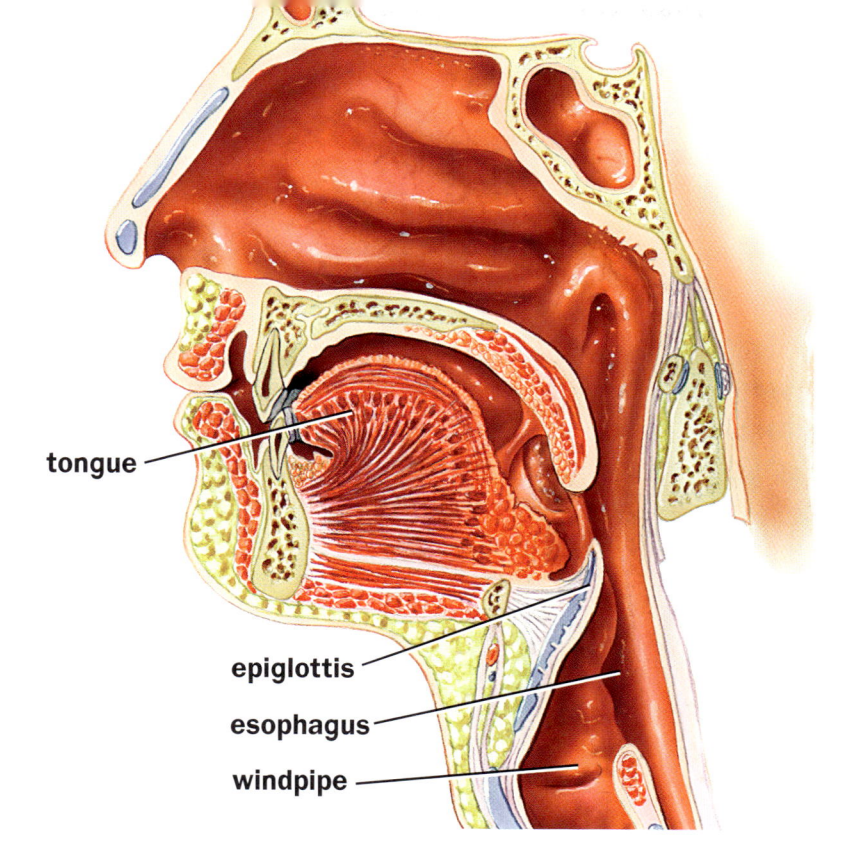

    Those tempting smells that drift from the kitchen at dinnertime trigger the salivary glands to start working. If you are hungry and catch a whiff of your favorite meal, before long you may notice you are salivating. As a matter of fact, you might even say digestion begins with the sense of smell!

    Chewing breaks the food down into smaller and smaller pieces so it can be swallowed easily. The tongue also helps mash the food around in the mouth. Then the tongue pushes the food to the back of the throat and you swallow. When you swallow, the chewed-up food goes down a ten-inch tube in the back of your throat called the esophagus. The windpipe, which receives the air you breathe in, also begins in the back of the throat. But your body has a special flap called the epiglottis that closes up the windpipe while you are swallowing and makes sure the food goes down the right tube. How does food then get down the esophagus? Muscles squeeze the walls of the esophagus, pushing the mashed food farther and farther down. After a few seconds, this squeezing motion has pushed the food down into the stomach.

The stomach is shaped like the letter *J*. It is sort of like a stretchy sack that expands when you eat a lot. Very strong stomach acids, called gastric juices, continue to digest the food even more. These acids are so strong that they could actually create a hole in the stomach wall. This usually does not happen, though, because the stomach also makes a thick mucus. This slimy substance helps protect the stomach walls and also helps churn the food. After about six hours in the stomach, food has become a thick liquid. Now it is ready for the next step in the digestion process.

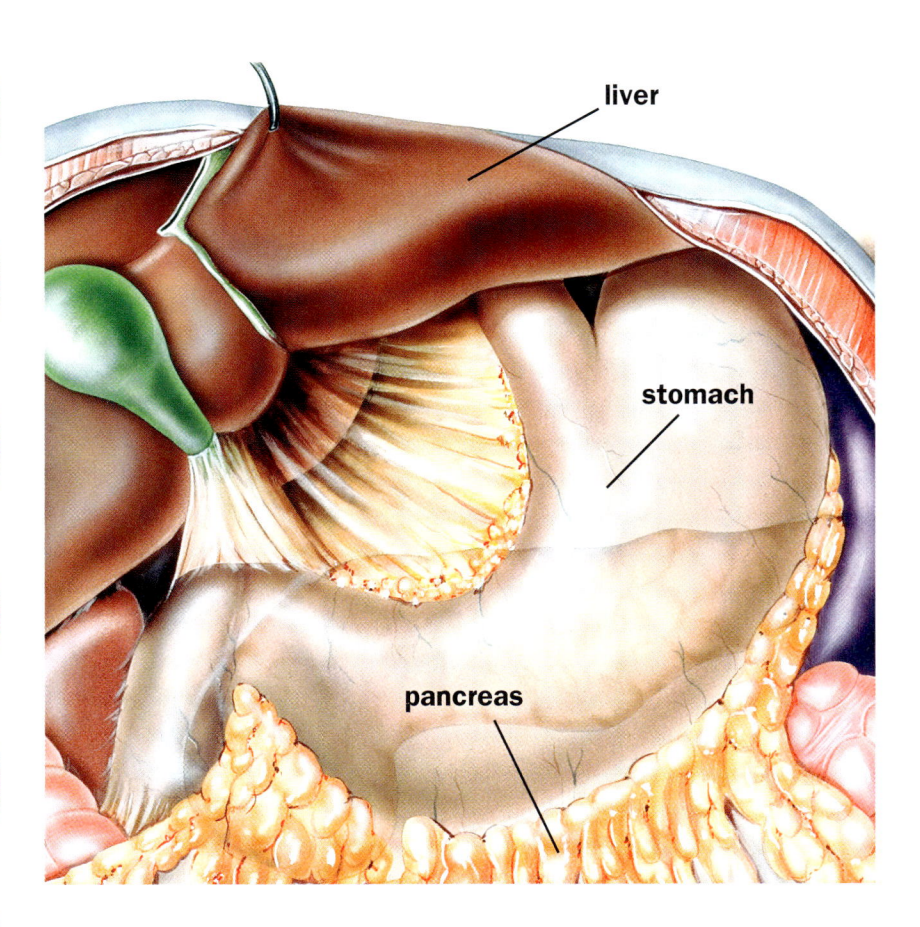

small intestine

large intestine

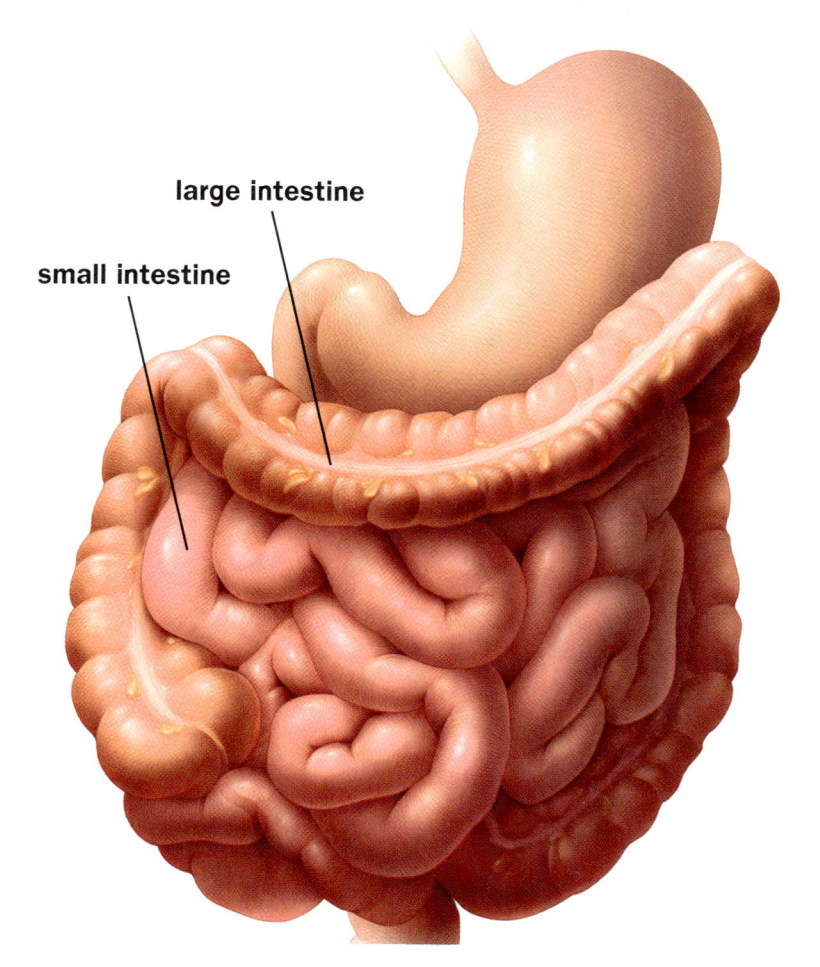

Next, the food enters another tube, which is the small intestine. It is very long and coiled around your insides below the stomach. If you stretched out an adult's small intestine, it would be around twenty feet long! The small intestine produces juices that help break down food even more.

At this point, digestion gets help from some other organs in the body that contribute their juices to the small intestine. The liver produces a substance called bile that helps break down fats so they can be absorbed into the bloodstream. Another organ, the pancreas, produces liquids that also help break down fats, proteins, and carbohydrates. Food has now been reduced to tiny, microscopic pieces. It is actually a thin liquid by now, and as it travels through the walls of the small intestine, all those fats, carbohydrates, minerals, vitamins, and proteins can be taken up by the bloodstream. The blood travels to every part of the body, supplying cells with these nutrients. But wait—there is more!

Next, the food that is not broken down and absorbed in the small intestine goes into the large intestine. The large intestine is not as long as the small intestine but still can stretch out to about five feet. That is as long as the average person is tall! The large intestine is filled with good bacteria that help break down food even more. The bacteria can be quite noisy when they are doing their job. Sometimes they bubble and make gas that your body releases as . . . well . . . gas. The large intestine also absorbs a lot of water while it holds the food your body does not use or need.

About eighteen to thirty hours after you eat something, the food that did not get digested is ready to leave the large intestine in a solid form. The body has taken all the nutrients it can from your dinner, and your food has been transformed to fuel for riding your bike, playing soccer, or even doing your homework. The next morning, when your stomach rumbles and you dash to the kitchen for some cereal, the process of digestion begins once again.

Unit 3

Focus Question What is it like to have a sprain or broken bone?

Ouch!

by Ann Dixon
illustrated by Mark Schroder

Yellow, purple, green, and blue—
lovely colors
except when you
watch them spread across your ankle
which is sprained and swollen,
a mass of congealed
vessels and veins
you'd prefer were not real
but won't go away
till the ankle has healed.

It's not much fun
and it's never fair
but neither is spraining
an ankle quite rare.
So moan if you like
and fuss if you dare
but till it's all better
you'd better take care.
So properly ice it
and properly prop it.
Sit back and relax
cause you've got to stay off it!

From Head to Toe

Poetry Reflections

These questions can help you think about the poem. Write your answers. Then talk about them with a partner.

- What advice does the speaker offer for someone with a sprained ankle?
- This poem deals with a part of a body system you have read about in this unit. Which system is that?
- Have you ever sprained an ankle or broken a bone? What did you have to do to recover?

Unit 3

Reading Reflections

These questions can help you think about the stories you read. Write your answers. Then talk about them with a partner.

Focus on the Facts

- Think about "From Food to Fuel." There are two types of substances in your stomach. Name them, and explain what they do.
- Janet tells about the hammer, the anvil, and the stirrup in "Can You Hear Me?" Where are these body parts? How did they get their names?
- Why do you think Elizabeth Blackwell worked so hard to become a doctor in "Graduation Day"?

Focus on the Stories

- Elizabeth Blackwell had to overcome many obstacles to become a doctor. Name a character in another story who overcomes obstacles.
- "What's That Smell?" explains that tiny hairs in the nose protect people from dirt and germs. Think about information in the other stories. Tell about tiny hairs in another part of the body. What is their job?
- "The Skeleton—Top to Bottom" explains that muscles move human legs and arms. These muscles may be familiar to you. But "More Than Meets the Eye" tells about unfamiliar muscles in human eyes. Tell about these muscles and how they work.

From Head to Toe

Focus on the Theme

- All our separate body parts actually work together as a team. Explain how two parts from different stories work together.
- Imagine a person is sleeping and there is a fire in the next room. Explain how something from four different stories might help him or her notice the danger and escape.
- What was the most surprising thing you learned from this unit's stories?

Focus Questions How did the Polunesians find their way at sea? Why might they be the greatest navigators?

The Great Navigators... And the Greatest

by Harold Wu

Imagine being in a boat and drifting away from the shore. Suddenly you lose sight of land. How do you find your way back? The problem is ages old. For thousands of years, sailors had to keep land in sight for fear they might never return. But slowly, people learned to navigate, or to find their way around while at sea.

At first, ship captains navigated by dead-reckoning. This means they learned and remembered all they could about wind, tides, and currents, using this information to get from one place to another safely. Keeping track of the stars was another good way for sailors to monitor their position on the sea. These celestial bodies were like signposts in the sky. The star Polaris, for example, always shows where north is.

But what about cloudy nights? How could they navigate then?

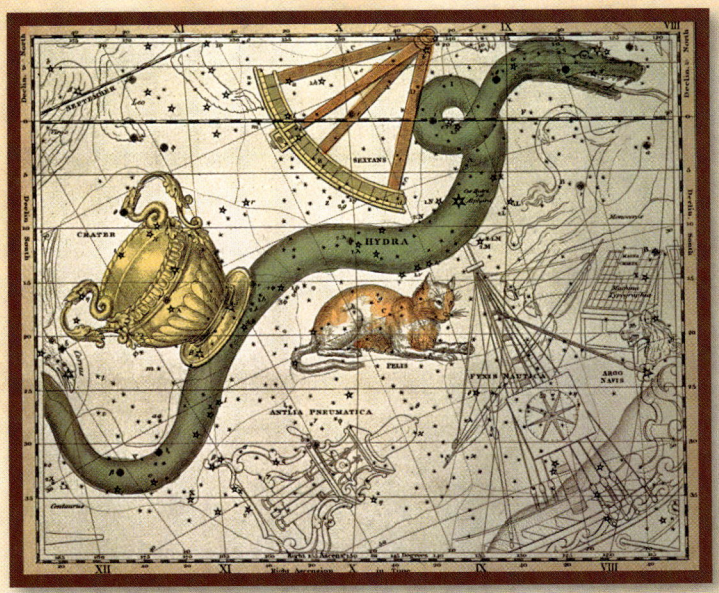

A page from an atlas of constellations

Around A.D. 300, the Chinese invented the very helpful compass, whose magnetic needle always pointed north. Later, Europeans invented other navigational instruments and good clocks for more accurate readings. Fewer sailors were lost at sea. Today, of course, satellites beam signals to global-positioning units. On land or at sea, they tell exactly where you are.

A few hundred years ago, those who could sail long distances were lauded as heroes. Columbus, Drake, Cook, and others were considered great navigators. But were they the greatest ever? What if they had had only canoes instead of ships? And what if they had had no compass, no clock, no map or chart? Sailors like that would be heroes indeed!

Those sailors really lived, but far to the west of America. They were the peoples of Polynesia who lived on the islands of Fiji, Tonga, and Samoa. These islands lay in the vast Pacific Ocean, which covers one-third of Earth.

Always close to the sea, the Polynesians sailed and fished every day, often far from land. And when there were too many people for their islands, they sailed in search of new islands. Hundreds of years before Columbus, they settled islands spread out over ten million square miles! What was their secret? There are two answers to that question: the double canoe and amazing navigational skills.

The double canoe was a key invention. It offered a more practical alternative to the basic canoe, which was narrow and easily tipped over. The resourceful Polynesians carved long canoes out of tree trunks using pieces of stone, bone, and coral. Then they put two canoes side by side and tied crossbeams over their hulls to make a double canoe. This vessel would not tip over or sink, even if both hulls filled with water. Better still, the crossbeams could support a deck, where people and goods could be loaded. The double canoe also carried a mast and a sail, which made it especially safe and fast. In fact, a crew member with Captain Cook, the English explorer who sailed to the Hawaiian islands, once remarked that a Tongan boat could sail "three miles to our two."

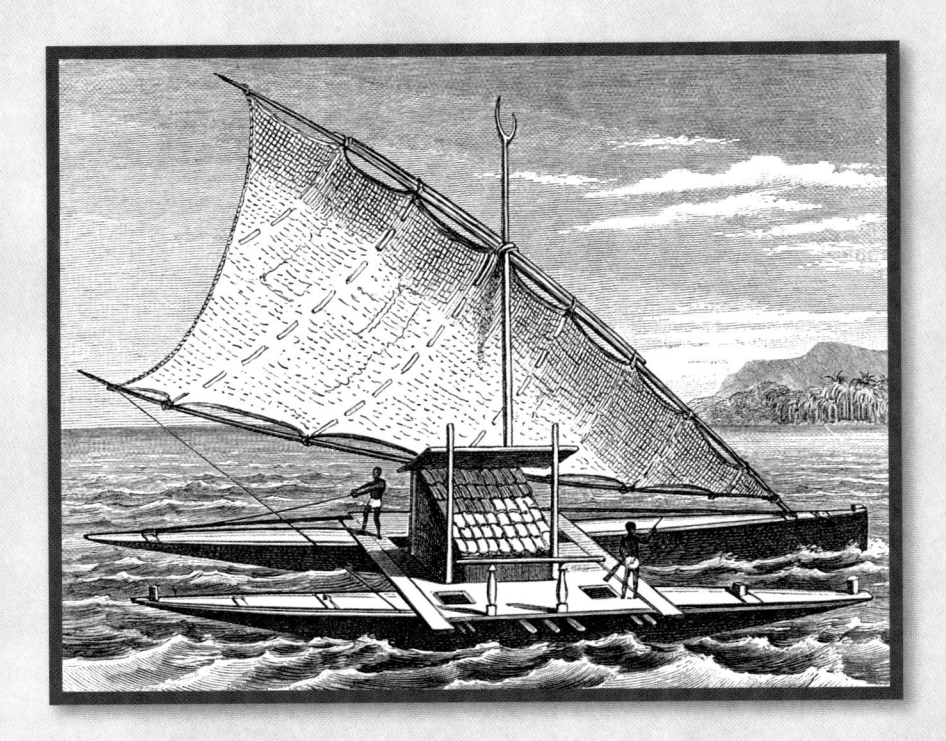

But even with good boats, the Polynesians still needed to find their way around. How did they do it with such success? First they memorized the positions of the stars and planets with the help of age-old stories passed down by word of mouth. They also noticed changes in the weather. If it got cold, for example, they surmised they might be too far north or south. Amazingly, they also kept track of time, even without the aid of clocks.

The Polynesians knew to watch for certain animals on their journeys that would offer clues about their position. A land-dwelling bird would tell them an island was nearby. These skilled sailors also noticed floating leaves, branches, or other signs of nearby land. They looked for clouds they knew would usually form over land. They learned what changes in the color of the daytime sky might mean.

These navigational skills enabled Polynesian sailors to travel thousands of miles over open ocean. But these voyages took great courage too. Storms could break boats to pieces and winds could tear sails to shreds. Hidden rocks could smash canoe hulls as well. Even in warm places, stormy nights could be brutally chilling. And without enough rain or enough fish to catch, the sailors could die of thirst or starvation.

Yet the hardy Polynesians braved everything. Around 300 B.C., they settled the area now called the Marquesas Islands. About six hundred years later they discovered and settled Easter Island, one of the most remote places on Earth. Around A.D. 400, they settled the Hawaiian Islands, and about the year 1000, they settled New Zealand.

A European map of the Pacific from the 1500s

A few years ago, some scientists concluded that all these Polynesian journeys must have happened by accident. Others decided to test this idea. They built a double canoe for sailing. And though no one knew how to navigate in the old way of the Polynesians, one traditional sailor said he would try. By dead-reckoning alone, he sailed from Hawaii to Tahiti—thousands of miles apart—and back again! The test left no doubt. The world's greatest navigators needed no compass or satellite. They had the best instruments of all: their own good minds and brave hearts.

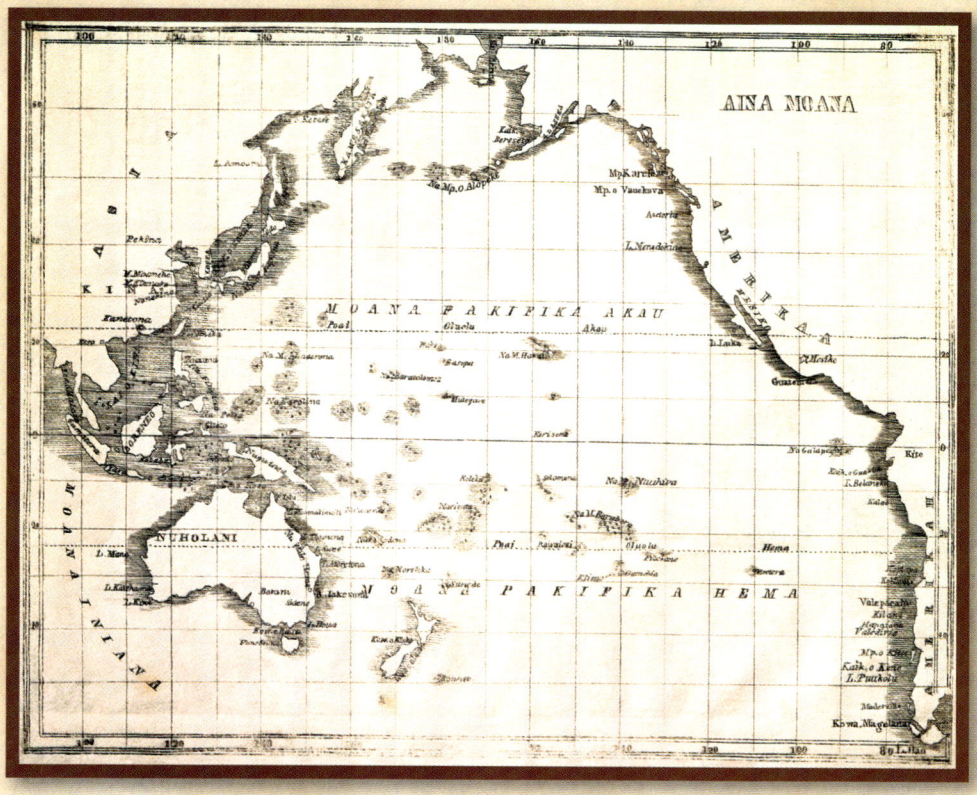

A map of the Pacific from the 1800s

Focus Questions Why are the people so alarmed by Columbus's boats? Why has Columbus come to their island?

Strangers on the Horizon

by Marta Leal

illustrated by Roberta C. Morales

At first they were merely small dots on the horizon. My sister and I noticed them as we were gathering palm leaves for weaving baskets. Perhaps they were large canoes, we thought, cutting through the waves from a neighboring island. People often visited our island, Guanahani, to trade goods and information.

But as these tiny specks came closer, they grew and grew in size. My sister and I dropped our palm leaves and glanced at each other in disbelief when we realized they were not canoes but much larger vessels. The sailing crafts looked to be made of wood and were as tall as several men standing on each other's shoulders. They seemed to have tree trunks rising from their middles with solid white clouds billowing ahead of them in the wind. When I squinted, I could just make out the shapes of people scurrying about on the top of the vessels.

Without another word, my sister and I took off into a sprint along the sandy path to our village. As we approached the stone-paved square, we could see dozens of people milling about, the same looks of shock on their faces we had had minutes before. Word of the strange sailing vessels had obviously spread.

I saw my father, who was one of the village elders, make his way into the chief's house. We followed him and peeked through the entryway at the men gathered on the hard dirt floor. They were all talking excitedly and gesturing wildly at each other. Then suddenly a young man who had been keeping watch on the ships ran in, shouting. The men on the giant vessels were lowering small canoes into the water and paddling straight for the shore!

The chief brought the alarmed council to order, and a hurried plan was formulated. A small group of elders, including the chief, would meet the approaching men on the beach. They would offer gifts of fruit, stone bowls, and baskets to the strangers to show they welcomed them in peace. Our people did not wish to have conflicts with others.

My sister and I tried to attract our father's attention; we wanted to follow the men to the beach. But a severe look from him soon destroyed our hopes. There was another way, however. While the men gathered their gifts, we snuck through the palms to a secret vantage point on a small hill above the beach. As we crouched down behind a bush, we could see one of the strangers' small canoes ride the surf and scrape along the sand before coming to a stop.

The men were very peculiar indeed—like none we had ever seen before. They were pale and weary-looking and covered from head to toe with an odd sort of clothing. As soon as their boat lodged itself into the shore, they lunged onto the sand with cries of joy and relief. Just how long had they journeyed, we wondered, in those giant vessels?

One man actually fell to his knees and kissed the sand as if it were a long-lost brother. This man, who seemed to be the group's leader, then struggled back to his feet and advanced on wobbly legs toward our chief. Both men greeted each other with their own tongues, and it was immediately apparent that a crude language of hand gestures would be needed for communication. The one thing we could understand was the stranger's name seemed to be Columbus.

We gathered from Columbus's sign language and the ragged appearance of his men that they had come a long way across a vast sea. It seemed he was looking for new people to trade with. Columbus was impressed with the gifts our chief then presented him. He even eyed with admiration the bits of gold our chief wore around his neck. Finally, I could see my father and the other elders breathe a sigh of relief.

But just what did the coming of these strangers mean for our people? Would Columbus trade peacefully with us? Would he want to live on our island? Would more of his people come in towering boats from across the ocean? My sister and I could only wonder.

Focus Questions Why does the narrator want to know about the Vikings? What does he find out?

Just Who Were These Vikings?

by Marcus Fyle
illustrated by Denny Bond

I had never even heard of Vikings until last week when I started summer tennis practice for my new junior high school. I spied the fierce-looking warrior in the horned helmet on my warm-up jacket and asked, "Hey, Coach, what is that?"

"Our mascot is the Viking," he said. "You know about Vikings, right? They were those explorers who practically took over the world a long time ago. They were from Norway, or was it Sweden? I can't remember. Anyway, ask Ms. Mata, the world history teacher. She'll tell you everything you want to know. Now let's get back to drills!"

Sure, I could go to Ms. Mata tomorrow, I thought, but I wanted to know right away. Luckily, Mom and I were supposed to visit my Aunt Suzanne, an ancient history professor at the local college, that very evening. I could ask her to give me the story. After all, if she could not tell me about these Vikings, then no one could.

"I must call on your great expertise, Aunt Suzanne," I said a few hours later, as I helped my aunt clear the dinner dishes from her table. "Who were the Vikings?"

"Ah, the Vikings," she said in her most professorial voice. "Those hearty northern Europeans famed for their long voyages."

"Yes, I think so," I replied. "They were explorers, right? When did they live, and where did they come from? My coach said Norway . . . or Sweden."

"Well, your coach is right. They came from Norway, Sweden, and Denmark. They made their explorations from about A.D. 800 to 1000," said Aunt Suzanne, pointing to a cozy couch in her study where we could sit and continue our conversation.

We sat on the couch, and Aunt Suzanne called to Mom in the other room and told her we would be awhile. "Those are some rather cold places, but they seem nice. Why did the Vikings want to find new lands?" I asked.

"They ran out of living space," answered Aunt Suzanne. "Around 800 was a time of global warming when the great snow fields melted and more land could be used for growing food and grazing cattle. More children grew to adulthood, and they had large families. Soon there were too many people."

"Really? There wasn't enough room for everyone?"

"Well, not technically. But Norse laws stated that a family's land could be passed only to the oldest son, so many young men had nowhere to live. They left for other places."

"And how did they travel?"

"The Vikings were great sailors and navigators," my aunt said, pointing to a painting on her wall of a long wooden ship. "They had longships and 'dragon ships' with savage animals painted on them. They knew a lot about getting around at sea. By keeping track of landmarks and the movements of the stars, they could set a course whatever the season, weather, or time of day."

"So, what lands did they discover?" I continued.

"Well, for one thing they are believed to have made it to North America long before the days of Christopher Columbus. They traveled from one island to another, setting up bases along the way. They made their way west and stopped at Finland, Iceland, Greenland, and other islands. They ended up in Newfoundland, a place on the coast of Canada." Aunt Suzanne pointed out the places on her big atlas as she talked.

"Do we know the names of any of these Vikings?" I asked.

"Yes, one very famous Viking was known as Erik the Red."

I chuckled and said, "Why? Was he red? Was he embarrassed to be a great explorer?"

"No, silly," Aunt Suzanne said, slapping me lightly on the shoulder. "He had red hair and a red beard. Erik started a settlement on the island of Greenland in the 980s."

"Greenland is rather far north. Was it really green there?" I asked, wrinkling my forehead.

"The name was very misleading. Even in those 'warm' years it was very cold. Farming was difficult. But Erik was trying to get others to settle there. So he called the place *Greenland* to make it seem nicer."

"That's not very honest," I said. "So, who was the one who discovered Newfoundland?"

"That was Erik's son, Leif Eriksson. He landed in North America around 1000 and set up the only permanent Viking settlement."

"Are the Vikings still there?"

"No, they sailed back home a few years later. We don't know why, but some may have fallen ill, or food may have been scarce. Native Americans may have driven them away—or maybe they were just lonely for friends and families."

"So where else did the Vikings travel?" I asked.

"They settled in Ireland, France, and other parts of Europe. In fact, the French region of Normandy is named for these Norse people. They also traveled to Italy and other Mediterranean lands, and they did lots of trading along the Volga River in what is now Russia. From the north they brought furs, walrus ivory, ropes, honey, and other goods. They bartered, or traded, them for spices, silks, and other things they couldn't get at home."

Suddenly Aunt Suzanne was interrupted by a tapping on the doorframe. Mom was standing in the doorway with a look that said it was time to go home.

"I have to ask one more thing, Aunt Suzanne," I said, putting on my jacket. "Those horned helmets—what were those all about? Did the Vikings really wear them all the time?"

Aunt Suzanne's whole body shook with laughter. "Oh, no," she said. "It would have been pretty difficult to keep those cumbersome things on their heads all day. While the Vikings may have had such hats for ceremonies, the idea that they wore horned helmets is purely a legend."

Aunt Suzanne was still wheezing with laughter as Mom and I drove off. Mom was a little annoyed at the late hour, but I was satisfied. While I would not be the best server for the Fairmont Vikings, I certainly would now be the foremost expert on the team's mascot.

Focus Questions Why did Zheng He make his voyages? Why was he so successful?

The Seven Voyages of Zheng He

by Helen Forrest

Vasco da Gama, James Cook, and Francisco Pizarro are the star explorers of today's history books. They sailed to lands where their countries—Portugal, England, and Spain—set up colonies and became rich and powerful.

But what about China? China has always been one of the world's biggest and strongest countries, but most people think no explorers ever lived there. They could not be more wrong!

Back in the late 1300s, a boy named Zheng He (Jeng Hay) was born. He became a servant of the Chinese emperor. He grew into a large man of well over six feet tall and proved to be a skilled, fearless sailor. The emperor put him in charge of the whole Chinese navy.

Francisco Pizarro

Zheng He commanded a mighty fleet with sixty-two treasure ships, called junks. It also had ships for troops, horses, supplies, trade goods, and water. With more than 300 ships and around 30,000 men, the entire fleet was like a floating city. The treasure ships were far bigger than any from Europe. They were up to 600 feet long and 150 feet wide! (Columbus's *Santa Maria* was tiny by comparison at less than 100 feet in length.) Some of the Chinese ships even had nine masts. Until centuries later, when steel came in to use, no European or American ship was ever this large.

A statue of Zheng He

Other ships supported the massive junks. Each had a special purpose:

- *Horse ships* carried trade goods and repair materials for the fleet.
- *Supply ships* held food for animals and the crew.
- *Troop transports*, six-masted ships, carried soldiers and arms.
- *Warships* protected the fleet from pirates and other enemies.
- *Patrol boats*, each with eight oars, brought people from one ship to another.
- *Water tankers* each carried about a month's supply of fresh water.

These ships had sails made of bamboo, which was woven into sturdy mats. Better still, these junks could sail "close to" the wind. This meant they were pushed along by wind blowing from the side, or even the front, so they could steer in many different directions. In contrast, European ships were square rigged. They had to keep the wind at their backs, steering wherever it blew them. This meant the Chinese could reach places other explorers could not.

Zheng He traveled tens of thousands of miles. He went on seven long voyages, sailing halfway around the world from China. First he visited the many lands of Asia, and then he went west to Africa, India, and even Egypt. Some even think he landed in America in 1421—seventy-one years before Columbus—but this has never been proved.

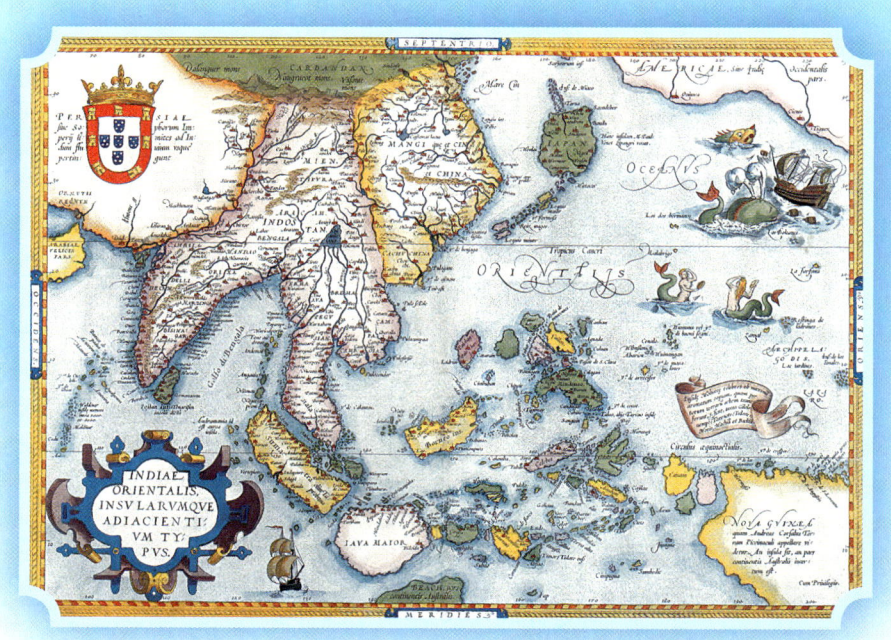

An early map of Asia

For nearly thirty years, the huge Chinese fleet journeyed to ports around the Indian Ocean. The ships carried silk, fine furniture, and fancy vases and dishes, which Zheng He exchanged for goods sold by Arab and African traders. These traders gave Zheng He spices, medicines, ivory, rare woods, and pearls.

But Zheng He's job was not to make money, for the emperor was already rich. Instead, he was sent to show off the power and majesty of China. He also brought back things considered rare and interesting. After visiting Africa, for example, he took aboard lions, leopards, "camel-birds" (ostriches), and zebras. After another voyage he brought back a giraffe. Members of the Chinese court thought this strange creature was a kind of unicorn.

During his seventh voyage, in 1433, Zheng He died at the age of sixty-two. It was a fateful moment for China. Had its explorations continued, China might have started colonies as European nations had done, and Chinese culture would have spread throughout the world.

At that time, however, Mongols were getting set to invade China, and the emperor ordered an end to exploration. Rather than spend money on trade, he built up the Great Wall of China. The huge fleet shrank to one-tenth of its former size, and China's "Golden Age of Exploration" was over.

Zheng He's name lives on in history, of course. He remains China's greatest explorer. But his fame may not stop there. Some historians believe he was the model for the greatest explorer of fiction, a character in a legendary Persian story. Similar-sounding names, plus Zheng He's seven voyages, have convinced them he was the real-life Sinbad the Sailor!

The Great Wall of China

Focus Questions What lands did James Cook explore? Why might sauerkraut be the secret to his success?

Sauerkraut, the Secret to Sailing Success

by Matt Bernél
illustrated by Jim Spence

Characters
Aurora Borealis
Captain James Cook

Setting: *A newsroom at a modern television station.*

At Rise: *Aurora Borealis, a professionally dressed news reporter, sits on an interview set with the famous sea captain of the eighteenth century, James Cook. They sit facing each other in comfortable chairs with a coffee table between them. Cook is dressed in clothes appropriate for an eighteenth-century sea captain.*

BOREALIS *(Facing audience)*: This is Aurora Borealis from Eyewitness News. Today we're speaking with one of history's greatest explorers, Captain James Cook. In the 1760s and 1770s Cook sailed around the world—farther than any other European. *(Turning to address Cook)* Welcome to the show, Captain, and welcome to the twenty-first century!
COOK *(Bowing head at Borealis)*: It is a pleasure, madam, to be speaking with you today.
BOREALIS *(Smiling, then looking serious)*: Captain Cook, you commanded ships in the British Royal Navy. How exactly did you get that job?

COOK: As a boy I excelled at math, so I joined His Majesty's service and learned navigation and the fine art of cartography, or mapmaking.

BOREALIS: Clearly, you knew how to find your way around. Where did you sail?

COOK: My first long voyage was from England to Tahiti.

BOREALIS *(To audience)*: That's an island in the western Pacific. *(To Cook)* Why sail all the way across two oceans?

COOK: We were searching for a large continent in that area, but it turned out not to exist.

BOREALIS *(Loudly)*: Oh, that is unfortunate! What else did you see on that trip?

COOK: We sailed to New Zealand's two main islands.

BOREALIS: Yes, the waterway between them was named after you: Cook Strait.

COOK *(Raising eyebrows in surprise)*: Is that so? I must admit I am flattered and, frankly, quite pleased. I also mapped eastern and northern Australia. As a matter of fact, my ship hit the Great Barrier Reef and nearly sank.

BOREALIS: In 1772 you made a second voyage. Where was that?

COOK: At first we went south, this time to prove there was no large continent at the pole. *(Crossing arms on chest and slightly shivering)* My, but it was chilly!

BOREALIS: It certainly was! You know, you were the first person to enter the Antarctic Circle. But you were wrong; there's a big continent at the south pole called Antarctica.

COOK *(Looking shocked)*: How remarkable! It looked to me like nothing but ice. Anyway, we turned north and visited Easter Island, where the people had made wonderful statues. Then it was on to Tahiti again, Tonga, and some other places.

BOREALIS: And your third trip?

COOK: On my last voyage we went looking for the Northwest Passage.

BOREALIS *(Chuckling)*: Ah, yes. The Northwest Passage was the much-hoped-for route across all of North America by water. And, like everyone else, you were—

COOK: —wrong again. Kindly don't remind me. *(Pauses to drink from mug of water on coffee table)* But we did find many other places of interest, and we sailed all around the Americas, winding up in Alaska. Along the way I named the Sandwich Islands.

BOREALIS *(To audience)*: Today the Sandwich Islands are an American state called Hawaii.

COOK: What an odd name.

BOREALIS *(Looking and pointing at Cook)*: We think the names *you* devised were odd. What about Sandwich? *(Winks at audience)* Was that what you had for lunch that day?

COOK *(Defensively)*: Really, Ms. Borealis, don't be silly. They were named for the Earl of Sandwich, a person of great importance. *(Puts mug back on table)*

BOREALIS *(In a severe tone)*: All right, let's get serious again. Captain Cook, you were the first European to sail over such vast distances. Why was that?

COOK: Oh, the answer is simple: scurvy.

BOREALIS: You're referring to a disease that debilitated many sailors at that time.

COOK: You are correct. It was a terrible illness that caused spots to appear on your skin, your teeth to fall out, and your brain to lose all sense. You—

BOREALIS *(With disgusted expression and hands over ears)*: Please, please, spare us the horrible details!

COOK: Well then, I'll simply say it was always fatal. In 1499 Vasco da Gama lost two-thirds of his crew to scurvy. In 1520 more than 80 percent of Magellan's men perished.

BOREALIS: Doctors have discovered what caused scurvy—a lack of vitamins B and C. Humans and guinea pigs are the only animals that can't make these vitamins themselves.

COOK *(Shrugging)*: Well, I don't know what these "vitamin" things are. But we did find a cure for scurvy.

BOREALIS: And that was . . . ?

COOK *(In a matter-of-fact tone)*: Lime juice. Oh, and possibly sauerkraut.

BOREALIS: Fresh fruits, such as limes, contain lots of vitamin C. So you served the crew limes with their meals?

COOK *(Shaking head)*: They didn't like them much. Sailors always want the same things to eat: salt beef and hardtack, which is a kind of biscuit.

BOREALIS (With confidence): So your men did eat limes. In fact, even today, British sailors are called "limeys" because of that.

COOK: Hmmm . . . how fascinating.

BOREALIS: But, of course, limes don't stay fresh for more than a week or two, so sauerkraut must have been the secret of your success.

COOK (Scratching head): Please explain.

BOREALIS (In the tone of an expert): Well, sauerkraut is just pickled cabbage, and cabbage is rich in vitamin C. The pickling process keeps the vitamin C in the cabbage, so crew members stayed healthy. Did they enjoy the sauerkraut?

COOK (Angrily): Certainly not. Sometimes my officers had to literally force them to partake of the briny spoonfuls!

BOREALIS *(Brightly)*: Even so, it worked wonderfully. You had hardly any scurvy aboard your ships, isn't that so?

COOK *(Nodding)*: Quite.

BOREALIS: And you succeeded where others had failed. *(Looks questioningly at Cook)* In fact, might we say that without sauerkraut you would not be the illustrious explorer you are today?

COOK *(With a sigh)*: If you must. *(Slumps down a little in seat and sighs again)*

BOREALIS: Thank you, Captain James Cook. *(Turns to audience with big smile)* We'll be back after this commercial break. *(Cook also turns to audience and gives a weak smile. Curtain closes)*

The End

Focus Questions How is Marco Polo thought to have impacted world exploration? Do you think the tales in his book are all true?

My Travels with Marco Polo

by Treyvon Grant
illustrated by Lindy Burnett

Marco Polo was seventeen years old when he left Venice with his father and uncle. Several years and thousands of miles later, they arrived at the summer palace of the ruler of the Mongolian Empire, Kublai Khan. Polo traveled for twenty-four years, and when he returned to Venice in 1295, it is said he had explored more of the world than any other person. For centuries, most of what Europe knew about the Far East came from the tales in Polo's book, The Description of the World.

In 1324, just before he died, Polo set free his Mongolian servant, Peter. Peter's account of his own life, as we might imagine it, must have been quite exciting as well.

I, Peter, have been a faithful servant to Marco Polo for the past fifty years. I was with him as he traveled within the Mongolian Empire. Then I followed him when he returned to Venice to live.

I am a Mongol. I was raised in the Land of Blue Sky, the high grassy steppes of Mongolia. My family lived in a white felt *ger*, a round tent (also known as a *yurt*). I grew up riding horses and herding sheep. The land is beautiful, but the climate is harsh. We moved our ger often to follow the grass and water for our animals.

Marco called me Peter, but my Mongol name is Dzoldzaya, which means "Light of Destiny." My father gave me this name because I was born at a time of great change in our family.

Genghis Khan conquered much of Asia and China and formed the vast Mongol Empire. His grandson, Kublai Khan, then became ruler of this empire. My father, Batkhuyag, which means "strong warrior," was Kublai's trusted advisor. I was fifteen when my father and I left the steppes and rode to the city of Khanbalig. I had never seen stone buildings or so many people in one place before.

Kublai Khan welcomed foreign traders. Niccolo and Maffeo Polo had been to China once before and now they had returned. They brought letters from the Pope and Niccolo's son, Marco. The Khan took a liking to the young Marco, and I was assigned to serve him.

Marco called me Peter and taught me to read and write. He spoke four languages and had no fear of trying different foods and customs. At ease when meeting new people, he was also an excellent storyteller.

We journeyed throughout the Empire. I saw how the Chinese farmers changed the land to meet the needs of the towns and cities. In contrast, the Mongols mastered living with the land as it was. I understood how the well-trained Mongol warriors were able to overtake the Chinese farmers.

The Khan built granaries for the poor and lowered taxes. He extended the Grand Canal and created postal stations. The Khan supported artisans and merchants. He funded advances in medicine and astronomy. He also relied on foreign advisors such as the Polos.

Even with all his power and wealth, the Khan never lost his love for Mongolia. On a trip north to my homeland, Marco and I were to gather seeds of the steppe grass. Upon our return to the Khan's palace, I planted the seeds in the palace courtyard. The Khan wanted to be reminded of the grass and blue sky of his youth on the steppes. Even the elegant summer palace, large enough to seat six thousand for a meal, was made of cane and two hundred silk cords. It could be taken down and moved like a ger on the grassland.

When Kublai Khan reached his seventies, the Polos thought it wise to return to Venice. The Khan, of course, did not want them to leave. He finally agreed to send them on a mission to deliver the Mongol princess, Kokechin, to Persia, where she was to marry the king. He gave them a golden tablet passport to ensure safe travel through areas of bandits.

The sea voyage to Persia was a wonder in itself. The endless waves of water reminded me of the waves of grass on the steppes. Our voyage was a success in that we delivered the Mongol princess. The king had died, but fortunately his daughter was wed to the Persian king's son, and the two countries remained allies.

We learned of the death of Kublai Khan in Persia. Luckily, his protection outlived him. The golden passports allowed us to travel back to the Black Sea unharmed. From there we traveled by ship to Venice.

In his homeland, Marco told tales of his amazing journey. He dictated his stories to Rustichello, the writer. Books were handwritten, each one taking a long time to make. Marco's tales were so popular that hundreds of copies were made of *The Description of the World*.

Marco brought asbestos cloth that did not burn and paper money from the Far East. His book tells of wondrous places, animals, foods, and customs. Many Venetians were reluctant to believe there were crocodiles and coconuts. These were things they had not seen with their own eyes. The story of the long-haired sheep of the Pamirs with horns seventy-five inches long seemed unreal. The legend of the elephant bird of Madagascar was doubted too. Yet as Marco said on his deathbed, "I have only told the half of what I saw."

Our grand adventure opened the eyes of the West to the wonders of the East. Kublai Khan welcomed foreigners and made travel safer on the Silk Road. In these ways, the Khan helped to usher in the new age of exploration. I predict that the curiosity sparked by Marco's book will inspire others to seek new routes to the Far East.

After being freed by Marco, I returned to my home in Mongolia by way of the Silk Road. I was finally reunited with my family and tribe. I told them of our wondrous journey from the eyes of a Mongol native. Once again, Kublai Khan enabled me to arrive safely. In his great wisdom, he had trees planted along the routes to mark the way in the winter snows.

Peter would never know just how accurate his prediction was. Polo's writings encouraged Columbus on his quest to find a sea route to the East. It is even said that Columbus carried a copy of Polo's book with him on his voyages.

Unit 4

Focus Questions Have you ever used a map for traveling? Was it helpful?

Maps

by Dorothy Brown Thompson
illustrated by Jesse Reisch

High adventure
    And bright dream—
Maps are mightier
    Than they seem:

Ships that follow
    Leaning stars—
Red and gold of
    Strange bazaars—

Ice floes hid
    Beyond all knowing—
Planes that ride where
    Winds are blowing!

Train maps, maps of
    Wind and weather,
Road maps—taken
    Altogether

Maps are really
    Magic wands
For home-staying
    Vagabonds!

Charting a Course

Poetry Reflections

These questions can help you think about the poem. Write your answers. Then talk about them with a partner.

- The speaker says that maps are "mightier / Than they seem." How can a map be mighty? What can it do for us?
- The poem mentions ships that follow stars as guides. Name some people you have read about in this unit who used the stars to navigate.
- At the end of the poem, the speaker suggests that studying maps can make us feel as though we are traveling the world. Do you think this is true? Why or why not?

175

Reading Reflections

These questions can help you think about the stories you read. Write your answers. Then talk about them with a partner.

Focus on the Facts

- Think about the end of "Strangers on the Horizon." Which of the chief's possessions does Columbus especially admire? What do you think that says about Spain's reasons for exploring?
- Think about "Sauerkraut, the Secret to Sailing Success." How did sauerkraut save the lives of Cook's sailors? Does Cook understand why the sauerkraut worked?
- Think about "Just Who Were These Vikings?" What was the original motivation for the Vikings' explorations?

Focus on the Stories

- Think about "The Great Navigators . . . And the Greatest" and "Just Who Were These Vikings?" Compare and contrast the Polynesian and Viking explorers.
- In "My Travels with Marco Polo," Peter says he thinks Marco Polo's book will inspire many new voyages. Do you think Zheng He in "The Seven Voyages of Zheng He" knew of Polo's book? Would it have inspired him? Explain your answer.
- Think about "Sauerkraut, the Secret to Sailing Success" and "The Seven Voyages of Zheng He." Contrast Captain Cook and Zheng He's reasons for exploring.

Charting a Course

Focus on the Theme

- Make a time line comparing some dates of each explorer's travels.
- Think about how each explorer from the stories traveled. What did they all have in common? Do you think modern explorers travel in different ways?
- Imagine someone has discovered a new island in the Pacific Ocean. Would you like to be in that group of explorers? Why or why not?

Focus Questions What instruments make up a mariachi band? How has the mariachi band changed through the years?

Mariachi!

by Stan Martin

What do you get when you combine trumpets, violins, one Spanish guitar, a guitar called a *vihuela*, and a bass guitar called a *guitarrón?* You get a lot of strings! You also get a lively band from Mexico called a mariachi band.

The mariachi band has its roots in a state in Mexico called Jalisco. In the early nineteenth century, groups of musicians began traveling from town to town performing in the streets. They played a variety of songs with their stringed instruments. Some were bright with a driving beat and syncopated notes. That means that instead of being with the beat, some of the notes were off, or between, the beat. Syncopation gave these songs an energy and an impact other tunes lacked.

Other mariachi songs were more like waltzes or polkas—popular dance melodies from Europe. Whatever the song, the sound of the mariachi bands was unique to this area of Mexico, combining traditional Spanish music with that of the native Mexicans. It could be only instrumental or it could be accompanied by singing.

Special dances could also accompany this spirited music. One example is a Spanish dance called the *zapateado*. It called for dancers to stomp the heels of their boots in quick, syncopated beats. Another dance known to many as the Mexican hat dance involves a male and a female dancer. These dancers perform carefully prescribed movements around a sombrero on the ground. The Mexican hat dance is now the national dance of Mexico.

The early mariachi musicians wore the clothes of a Jalisco peasant—simple white cotton trousers and shirts and sandals. They eventually came to perform in the town squares of Mexico, where more people could hear and appreciate their music. In the early 1900s certain bands became famous as mariachi music gained more respect. These were not just simple peasants plucking guitars. They were professional musicians singing the songs of Mexico.

A band led by Gaspar Vargas moved to Mexico City at this time. The band earned national fame—and an invitation from the president of Mexico to play at his inauguration. Vargas's band worked to write down the music they performed so others could play it. They also welcomed other musical influences from the United States and South America. They and other mariachi bands began to change their costumes during this period as well. They traded their humble garb for richly decorated jackets and pants, bow ties, boots, and sombreros.

As radio and motion pictures became widespread in Mexico, the popularity of the mariachi bands soared. The trumpet became a more important part of the group. Elements of jazz and Cuban music made their way into the mariachi tunes that could now be heard over the airwaves and in movie theaters. Mariachi musicians became stars of the silver screen—and eventually the television screen.

Today, mariachi music is one of the most recognizable parts of Mexican culture. Its driving rhythms entertain people within and beyond the borders of Mexico. So be on the lookout for musicians in fancy suits and sombreros. You can look forward to a festive, one-of-a-kind musical experience.

Focus Questions What instruments make up a bluegrass band? What does this kind of music mean to Connor and his family?

Blue Kentucky

by Shelly Porter
illustrated by Bradley Clark

The first time Connor could remember hearing bluegrass music, he was three years old. Blue Kentucky, the band his father and uncle had started, was playing to a small crowd at the park. Connor stood in front of the small wooden stage, bending his knees and stomping his feet to the rhythm. He could feel the music running through him like an electric current that made it nearly impossible to stand still.

His dad started him on the banjo the next year. Then Connor learned to play the harmonica from his older brother, Jesse. By the time Connor was seven years old, he regularly played and practiced with Blue Kentucky. The twang of the banjo, the trill of the fiddle, the steady thump of the bass—the notes of bluegrass music were the soundtrack to Connor's life.

Blue Kentucky practiced on Friday nights and sometimes on Sunday afternoons. They would take turns using the members' basements, garages, and backyards. If they were practicing for an actual performance, everyone took things a little more seriously. Connor's favorite practices, however, were the less organized ones when everyone played simply for the fun of it.

Jesse ran track, and he talked sometimes about "getting into the zone." That was the phrase he used to describe how it felt when he was running and everything else in the world seemed to fall away. All that was left was the pavement and his legs doing what they were meant to do.

Connor knew exactly what his brother was talking about. He experienced the same thing playing his banjo with the band. They would play a song, and everyone would take turns soloing while the others played backup. Connor would lose himself in the music, every fiber in his body vibrating with the cheerful beat. When the session ended, he saw that the others had journeyed to the same place he had just been. Somehow he was a member of a team and the only person in the world at the same time.

The summer Connor turned thirteen, his father was laid off from the factory where he had worked for almost two decades. The mood around the Greavey household slowly changed. It became obvious it was not going to be easy for Connor's dad to find more work. The factory had let a number of long-term employees go when part of its operations were moved overseas. So Mr. Greavey was not the only person in town looking for a job. The longer he went without finding anything, the quieter the Greavey house became.

When Mr. Greavey began canceling practices in the first few weeks after he was laid off, Connor assumed it was temporary. His mom explained that his father was going through a rough time and that the whole family was going to need to make some adjustments. Connor accepted this. But as the weeks wore on, he missed Blue Kentucky and his banjo more and more.

No one had told him he could not practice, but something about it felt wrong. Filling the somber house with the melody of "Blue Moon of Kentucky" or belting out a tune on the harmonica seemed disrespectful. If his dad had forsaken music for a time, Connor felt he ought to do the same.

One day in September, Connor came home from school to find his father sitting on the front porch. In his lap, he held his fiddle. His sun-browned hands rested against the yellow wood of the instrument's body.

"Hey, Dad," Connor said. He dumped his backpack on the floor and took a seat in one of the worn white rockers. "What are you doing?"

Mr. Greavey grinned, and Connor realized it had been months since he had seen a real smile on his dad's face. Without a word, he picked up his fiddle and began playing. Connor leaned back in the rocker and let the music wash over him. Mr. Greavey played for nearly an hour. When he finally laid the fiddle back in its case, Connor could see the relief on his face.

"You found a job, didn't you?" Connor asked, regretting the words almost as soon as they slipped from his mouth. If he were wrong, it would just make his dad feel worse.

"Not yet, Connor," Mr. Greavey said. "I just figured it was time I started playing again. It's been too quiet around here, don't you think?" He put one arm around his son's shoulders as they walked into the house and the screen door gently shut behind them.

Focus Questions What is the story behind the ballet *The Lake of Swans*? Why is the narrator so excited to see the ballet?

The Swans of the Bolshoi

by Melanie Sabato
illustrated by Johanna Van der Sterre

6 April 1877

Something quite amazing has happened. Mama has just received a letter from her sister, Nataliya. She has tickets for us all to see *The Lake of Swans* at the Bolshoi Theatre on the last day of this month!

Several girls at school have been to the ballet before, and I have done my best not to feel envious of their good fortune. I smiled when they told me about the tragic and romantic stories that unfolded on stage. I listened as they hummed the score and described the costumes and scenery. I even learned a little ballet myself by watching them imitate the dancers. Now it is my turn to see all this for myself.

2 May 1877

I do not know where to begin. Everything I have seen and heard in the last few days is swirling about in my mind. Mama, Papa, Sergei, and I left for Moscow early in the day. By the time we reached Aunt Nataliya's, I could barely bring myself to eat the midday meal she had prepared. The rest of the afternoon is a blur, but I remember quite clearly my first glimpse of the Bolshoi Theatre.

The most elegant-looking people I have ever seen milled about. They filled the fine marble halls with the clicking of their best shoes and the tinkling of their laughter. When we were seated inside the theater, I was surrounded by red and gold—just what I imagine it must be like to live at the imperial palace. Everything glinted and sparkled. The sounds of the orchestra tuning their instruments sent shivers down my spine.

Aunt Nataliya told me the music was composed by a brilliant man named Pyotr Ilyich Tchaikovsky. The story is based on a German legend that tells the tragic tale of Odette, a princess who is cursed by an evil sorcerer and turns into a swan.

The ballet premiered in February in this very theater, but it was not well received. It was not so much Tchaikovsky's music that was criticized but the choreography and performance. I do not have the most practiced eye, but to me it was magical. Even Aunt Nataliya, who has attended many such events, said she believed the dancers to be highly skilled and the music perfectly suited to the story. Perhaps the critics just needed something to write about.

Mama and I shared a program, and I made sure to pay attention to when each new movement or scene began. I wish I could have memorized every note that soared toward the ceiling in that grand theater. I wanted to remember the music that was paired with each dance so I could replay it all in my mind later.

It is probably no surprise that I was most impressed with the performance of Anna Sobeshchanskaya. She danced the role of Odette as well as Odile, the daughter of the sorcerer von Rothbart. You see, Prince Siegfried falls in love with Odette even though she has been cursed to live her life as a swan. Von Rothbart tries to deceive the prince by disguising his own daughter as Odette at a ball hosted by the prince. The only difference is that Odile wears black instead of white.

When the prince was fooled, my heart sank. I did not think he would make the mistake of choosing Odile. To my great relief, the true love of Siegfried and Odette triumphs.

Miss Sobeshchanskaya was so graceful, so confident. Her body looked nearly weightless. She expressed such joy and sadness through her dancing without ever uttering a word.

Aunt Nataliya told me after the performance that Miss Sobeshchanskaya had originally disliked certain parts of the ballet. She traveled to St. Petersburg, where ballet master Marius Petipa created a new *pas de deux*, or dance, for her. Tchaikovsky was rather angry about the whole episode. He insisted that he had to rewrite the score to accompany the new dance steps. I certainly do not know how Miss Sobeshchanskaya had the courage to make such a decision, but it seems as though she knew just what improvements needed to be made.

Perhaps the most memorable part of the evening for me came after the performance ended. Aunt Nataliya led us to Miss Sobeshchanskaya's dressing room and personally introduced me! I was too nervous to say much, aside from complimenting her on such beautiful dancing. If only I knew more about ballet. I wish I could have casually tossed around the French terms for the graceful moves I had seen Odette/Odile perform.

Before we left, Miss Sobeshchanskaya cupped my face in her hand. She told Mama and Aunt Nataliya that I had the body of a dancer. Those were her exact words—*the body of a dancer!* It was an evening I shall never forget.

Focus Questions How is the hula dance a part of Malia's heritage? What will she gain by learning to hula?

Island Homecoming

by Alma Lazo
illustrated by Stacy Schuett

    Malia sat on the front step of her grandmother's house watching the sun gradually inching higher into the sky. She heard the *shushing* of waves breaking along the shore in the distance, but all she could think of was how far Hawaii was from Portland, Oregon. Growing up in Portland, she had never considered living anywhere else. She knew her parents had been worrying about Tutu's health for a couple of years. It had not occurred to her, however, that they would all pack up and move to Hawaii to live with her grandmother.

Malia had thought moving to the islands might feel like a sort of homecoming. She had never lived there, but her parents had been born in Hawaii and had not migrated to the mainland until after college. The faces of the people she saw on the Hawaiian streets and the lilt in their voices were familiar. Yet somehow it was not enough to make Malia feel the connection she had hoped to find.

Malia sighed and went inside to shower and get dressed. A girl who lived down the street had invited Malia to take hula lessons with her. Malia agreed, figuring it might be a good way to meet some people before school started.

Later that morning, the two girls walked down the street toward the *halau*, or school of dance. "When you first asked if I wanted to take hula lessons, I thought you were kidding," Malia admitted. "I thought hula was just something performed for the benefit of all the tourists here."

Lanikai grinned and nodded. "I can see why it might have that reputation, but it's actually pretty important to our culture and history. Hawaiians didn't have written language until the 1800s. Hula was a way to pass on traditions and stories. I like the idea of being part of that chain of history. Needless to say, my parents were thrilled when I said I wanted to learn hula."

"So it's more than just a dance," commented Malia.

Lanikai nodded. "It's definitely more than that. The movements and music tell a story or describe something in nature. The traditional older form of hula was called *hula kahiko*. It was more formal and serious. The purpose was often to honor the king or pay tribute to gods and goddesses, so it was considered really offensive and even bad luck if you made a mistake. Imagine how stressful that would have been!" she exclaimed.

"The movement was faster, too, and more energetic," continued Lanikai, pausing to give Malia a quick sample of what she meant. "In *hula 'auana*, which is what we'll be learning, the *mele*, or chants, are sung to a melody. The gestures are softer and more relaxed." Lanikai swirled her hips and moved her arms in a slow liquid motion to illustrate.

"I'm amazed you know so much about this already," said Malia. She stopped to look at a small lizard sunning itself on a flowering bush. It blinked at her and disappeared into the lush greenery. The girls started walking again.

"Hula's kind of a big thing in my family," said Lanikai. "Did you know our grandmothers first met each other as girls when they danced hula together?"

"You're kidding!" exclaimed Malia. She had a hard time picturing Tutu—who was tiny and stooped and walked with a cane—swaying rhythmically and chanting ancient stories. "I'll have to remember to ask my grandma whether she has any pictures."

"On the other side of the family, my mom's mother was a *kumu hula*, which is like a hula master," Lanikai continued. "This stuff is definitely in my blood."

As the girls walked up the driveway to the halau, the cheerful melody of hula music poured through the open windows of the squat, coral-colored building.

"That's my dad and brothers practicing," said Lanikai. "Dad and Keoni play the ukulele. Akamu plays the steel guitar and occasionally the *pahu* drums. During lessons we'll probably practice to a CD, but they're going to play at our final performance."

"No wonder your family was excited when you said you wanted to get involved in hula," laughed Malia.

As the girls walked inside, their eyes adjusted to the change in light. When Malia could see again, she found herself staring at a man her dad's age wearing a colorful shirt. He nodded his head deeply and grinned, displaying the same dimple as Lanikai. Then he said something in the Hawaiian language.

"My dad's welcoming you," translated Lanikai. "He says that when one wants to dance the hula, bashfulness should be left at home. It's an old Hawaiian proverb."

Malia could not help smiling. Hawaii still might not feel like home, but between Lanikai and hula lessons, she had a suspicion it would not be long before it did.

Focus Questions What impact did Louis Armstrong have on the music of his day? What did he achieve?

Satchmo: One of a Kind

by Mara Loveland

Duke Ellington, Dizzy Gillespie, Ella Fitzgerald, Charlie Parker, Billie Holiday. No list of jazz greats would be complete without a tribute to the dynamic singer and musician Louis Armstrong. Often known as "Satchmo," Armstrong had enormous talent and a personality to match. His contributions to music changed the world of jazz. Just listen to one of his trumpet solos or his powerful singing voice, and you will know why Satchmo will live forever in the hearts of music lovers around the world.

New Orleans, birthplace of Louis Armstrong

    Armstrong's childhood in the early 1900s was not easy. His family was very poor, and his father was never really a part of his life. Armstrong, who was raised by his mother and grandmother, started working odd jobs when he was only seven. He dropped out of school before he even finished the elementary grades.

    Armstrong loved music from an early age. As a boy, he bought a cornet, a type of trumpet, with the help of a family he worked for. He taught himself to play and became a member of a brass band at a home for troubled boys where he was sent as a teenager. It was lucky that Armstrong lived in New Orleans. The city was known for being the birthplace of jazz, and jazz would turn out to be a lifelong passion for Armstrong.

King Oliver's Creole Jazz Band

During the next few years, Armstrong got his first taste of life as a professional musician. He played some gigs in local blues bands and on steamboats that traveled the Mississippi River. A famous cornet player named Joe "King" Oliver became a mentor to Armstrong. When Oliver moved to Chicago, Armstrong took his place in a popular New Orleans jazz band. Several years later, in 1922, Armstrong followed Oliver to Chicago and joined his Creole Jazz Band.

Chicago was an amazing place to be a musician in the 1920s. The city was alive with jazz music, and Armstrong quickly made a name for himself. He also spent some time in New York City, which was another popular place for jazz musicians of the time. Back in Chicago, he began recording under his own name with a band called the Hot Five.

Around this time, Armstrong started playing the trumpet instead of the cornet. He could make the instrument do things that few other people could. He practiced constantly, but he also had a natural talent for getting the trumpet to sing. Armstrong played popular music of the time as well as jazz standards, but he made each song his own. He and his band were known for their improvisation, or improv. They took a piece of music and changed it as they played, each person reacting to the music of the others.

Until the era of Armstrong, jazz was more of a team effort. The musicians in a band played together to produce a piece of music that worked as a whole. Armstrong's style of performing jazz was different because every musician had a voice. Each member of the band had a chance to express himself or herself as an individual. All the different pieces came together to form something exciting and new.

Armstrong sings with another jazz legend: Ella Fitzgerald.

    Armstrong's talent was not limited to playing the trumpet. He was also an incredible singer. His unique voice was deep, gritty, and hard to forget. After dropping the lyrics to a piece of music one day, he was encouraged to continue singing without it. This style of singing is called scatting. The singer treats his or her voice as an instrument, using various sounds and nonsense words in place of the lyrics during certain parts of a song. Armstrong was a master of scatting. The first record he produced featuring this style of singing was called *Heebie Jeebies*, and it quickly soared up the charts. Just like that, Armstrong popularized another new trend in the world of jazz.

Over the years, Armstrong continued to entertain his fans. He recorded with the biggest names in the business, including Bing Crosby, Ella Fitzgerald, Duke Ellington, and Bessie Smith. He was sponsored by the U.S. State Department and performed all around the world, traveling to Europe, Africa, and Asia. For much of his life, he played nearly every day of the year. Armstrong even went on to have a career in film. He was one of the first African Americans to regularly appear in major American motion pictures. During the course of his lifetime, Armstrong appeared in dozens of movies.

On July 6, 1971, at the age of sixty-nine, Armstrong died in New York City. The impact he had on jazz music and jazz singing made him a legend, but it was his big personality and passion for music that made the world fall in love with him. Armstrong was a classic—a one-of-a-kind musician and a fascinating human being.

Focus Questions How can a talent for music help people communicate? What are your talents?

A Musical Connection

by Mohit Bhatti

Everyone has special talents. Some people are whizzes at science while others have beautiful singing voices. Some can dunk a basketball. Others can make a room full of people laugh. Once in a while, though, a person is born with an extraordinary talent of some kind. It is even more impressive when it appears in a person who also has disabilities.

Autism is a condition in which people have trouble communicating with others. Many people with autism have limited speech. About 10 percent are savants. This means they have some sort of exceptional mental ability. For example, an autistic savant who has a talent for math may be able to solve very complex problems. Not all savants have autism, and not all people with autism are savants. But the two conditions sometimes occur together.

For some people with autism, music can have a powerful effect. Some are even musical savants. They may not connect to others with language, but music can bridge this gap in communication. It can even have the effect of opening up learning pathways and allowing them to gain new skills in many areas.

It is not really surprising that music has such amazing power. Music touches something very basic in most human beings. It does not matter who they are or where they come from. Long before there was written language, the traditions and stories of many cultures were passed on through music. It can be a common ground for people of different ages, beliefs, and backgrounds.

Specialists who work with musical savants have noticed they are driven to practice their special skill. It is an important part of their lives, and each day revolves around it. This certainly seems to be the case for a man named Tony DeBlois.

When DeBlois was born, he weighed less than two pounds. The life-saving treatments he needed soon made him unable to see. By the age of two, though, he showed an interest in music and began to play a toy piano. Today DeBlois is in his thirties and is a successful jazz musician. His first love is the piano. But he can also play many other instruments, including the organ, guitar, banjo, drums, and harp.

Tony DeBlois, right, accepts an award.

Anyone who has watched DeBlois perform has seen the joy music brings him. His face lights up, and he is filled with energy. He loves the applause of his audience—in his living room or a full auditorium. DeBlois knows more than eight thousand songs, but that is not the only thing that makes his talent so amazing. Some musical savants are only able to imitate the sounds they hear. DeBlois can improvise, or create changes that make a piece of music his own. This shows that DeBlois is good at more than just memorizing. He has a true understanding of music.

Another young musician, Brittany Maier, has a story that is similar in some ways to DeBlois's. She also has autism and has trouble communicating with words. Very early in life, though, Maier's parents saw that music could reach her in a way nothing else could. They also found that she was able to play the music from an entire CD after hearing it only a few times.

Today Maier is a teenager who is just as dedicated to the piano as ever. She knows more than fifteen thousand songs and adds about a thousand more each year. Since she was ten, Maier has also been composing her own music. This is something that seems to bring her much pleasure. Sometimes she spends as long as twelve hours a day at the piano. Music is the way Maier reaches the world around her. There is no doubt it is the passion of her life.

Experts are not exactly sure where the talent of musical savants comes from. Their families often do not include other super-talented musicians. One thing the doctors have noticed is that visual impairment, autism, and great musical talent all tend to go hand-in-hand in musical savants. The human brain is still a mystery in many ways. Studying the world of people like DeBlois and Maier might offer clues as to how important music is in helping them connect to others.

Focus Questions Have you ever heard African music? What did it make you think of?

Danse Africaine

by Langston Hughes
illustrated by Chris van Es

The low beating of the tom-toms,
The slow beating of the tom-toms,
    Low . . . slow
    Slow . . . low—
    Stirs your blood.
        Dance!

A night-veiled girl
    Whirls softly into a
    Circle of light.
    Whirls softly . . . slowly,
Like a wisp of smoke around the fire—
    And the tom-toms beat,
    And the tom-toms beat,
And the low beating of the tom-toms
    Stirs your blood.

To the Beat

Poetry Reflections

These questions can help you think about the poem. Write your answers. Then talk about them with a partner.
- The speaker describes a girl who "Whirls softly into a / Circle of light." What do you think she is doing?
- The poem describes a form of African music played on drums. Recall some of the other kinds of music and instruments you have read about in this unit. Make a chart that lists each kind of music and the instruments that are used to play it.
- The speaker says that the beating of the drums "[s]tirs your blood." What does he or she mean by this?

Unit 5

Reading Reflections

These questions can help you think about the stories you read. Write your answers. Then talk about them with a partner.

Focus on the Characters

- In "The Swans of the Bolshoi," what did Anna Sobeshchanskaya demand before she would perform *The Lake of Swans*? How did Tchaikovsky feel about it?
- Think about "Island Homecoming." Malia learns that hula was an ancient Hawaiian way of passing on traditions. How does hula help Malia learn about her people? Explain your answer.
- In "Mariachi!" what did mariachi bands originally wear? How and why did their costumes change?

Focus on the Stories

- In "Satchmo: One of a Kind," Louis Armstrong made the trumpet an important part of jazz. In what other type of music did the trumpet become more important during the 1900s?
- In "A Musical Connection," music is a way of communicating for some musical savants. Tell about another character who uses music or dance to communicate. What does he or she communicate?
- Compare and contrast mariachi bands from "Mariachi!" with bluegrass bands from "Blue Kentucky."

To the Beat

Focus on the Theme

- If you could learn to play one type of music from this unit, what would it be and why?
- Traditional types of music help us honor the cultures they come from. Tell about one character from this unit who uses music to honor his or her roots.
- In your opinion, which musician or dancer in the unit had to work the hardest to achieve his or her goals? Explain your answer.

Focus Questions Why does Cliff love windsurfing? What does he learn about loyalty?

The Very Best Sport

by Camilla York

illustrated by Paula Zinnegrabe Wendland

"Watch out!" yelled Grant.

It was too late. The soccer ball spun right into the side of Cliff's head.

"Oh . . . sorry," Cliff yelled back absentmindedly.

"What's going on?" Grant asked in an irritated voice. "You need to pay more attention. We need a lot more practice before this weekend's game."

Cliff and Grant were ninth graders on the island of Barbados in the eastern Caribbean Sea. They were playing soccer, one of the island's most popular sports for students. Cliff and Grant's team was doing well and was favored to win in the upcoming game, but Cliff's heart was not in it.

Since he had starting playing sports as a little boy, Cliff had always felt like he was being pushed in a direction he did not want to go. He had not liked cricket, the first sport he had attempted. Cricket is the national sport of Barbados, and almost everyone on the island plays. The man considered the world's greatest cricket player is from Barbados. Children are taught the game at a young age. Cliff, however, had found the game, which involves batting a ball and running between two stumps called wickets, quite boring.

When Cliff was a little older and his parents detected his lack of enthusiasm for cricket, they had suggested soccer. Millions of people around the world love the game, and Cliff was a good athlete, so it was natural for him to give it a try. Unfortunately for Cliff, he was good at it. It all came naturally to him, but it just did not excite him. Even now, when his team was headed for a championship, he could not keep his mind on it. Instead, Cliff dreamed of water, waves, and the big, warm winds of the Caribbean.

After practice Cliff ran straight home and grabbed his windsurf board, or sailboard. Windsurfing is a popular sport for natives and visitors to Barbados. Most students in Cliff's school, however, preferred the team sports of soccer, basketball, and, of course, cricket. Cliff could not understand their attitude. Windsurfing was the sport for him.

What was better than being out alone on the sea on your board, with the wind in your face, going so fast you felt you were flying? Cliff was learning some advanced maneuvers, such as gybying, turning downwind at speed; tacking, turning upwind; and jumping. Cliff had always been in good shape, but he knew he had to get in even better shape to perfect these moves. He started doing calisthenics every day: push-ups, sit-ups, and, his favorite, pull-ups. He was up to forty pull-ups in a row! The exercise was difficult, but one goal kept him moving. He needed to be strong and agile in order to maneuver the sail and the board, especially if he was going to compete in this sport someday.

After school the following day, Cliff stopped off at the local surfboard shop. He liked checking out all the new windsurfing equipment, even if he could not afford it. He could always dream about it, and maybe someday he would start winning competitions and earn enough money to actually buy all this stuff. And then he would compete in the Olympics!

As Cliff was about to leave, something on the wall caught his eye. A brightly colored brochure announced an upcoming amateur windsurfer competition. A small prize would be awarded to the first-, second-, and third-place finishers. Cliff was ecstatic. He knew he was ready for an amateur competition—and this could be his big break. He grabbed the brochure and started reading the details. "Oh, no," Cliff said aloud, "the competition is this Saturday, and the big soccer game is this Saturday too. Now what am I going to do?"

At first Cliff felt as if he could not really talk about this with his parents. How could they understand his dilemma when they really wanted him to become a big soccer star or the next cricket sensation? "Well that's never going to happen," laughed Cliff, "so I might as well tell them the truth."

After dinner that night Cliff told his parents about his dream of becoming a champion windsurfer, how he had absolutely no desire to play soccer or cricket, and about the windsurfing competition on Saturday. Cliff was surprised; his parents seemed only a little disappointed. His mom, of course, expressed her concern about the flips and turns and all the tricks he was doing on the sailboard, but Cliff assured her he was training properly. What they seemed most disappointed about was the problem of the soccer game on Saturday.

"Do you really want to let your team down, Cliff?" his father asked, looking directly into Cliff's eyes. "Think about Grant and your other friends. They've been practicing hard, and this is important to them."

"But the competition is important to me!" Cliff replied. As he said the words, however, he knew what he had to do. He had committed to the soccer team and the school. The windsurfing competition would have to wait, but not for much longer.

"I'll play in the game and support my friends," Cliff said. "But just wait until the next windsurfing competition. I'm going to show Barbados what I can do! And finally I'm going to compete at the very best sport there is!"

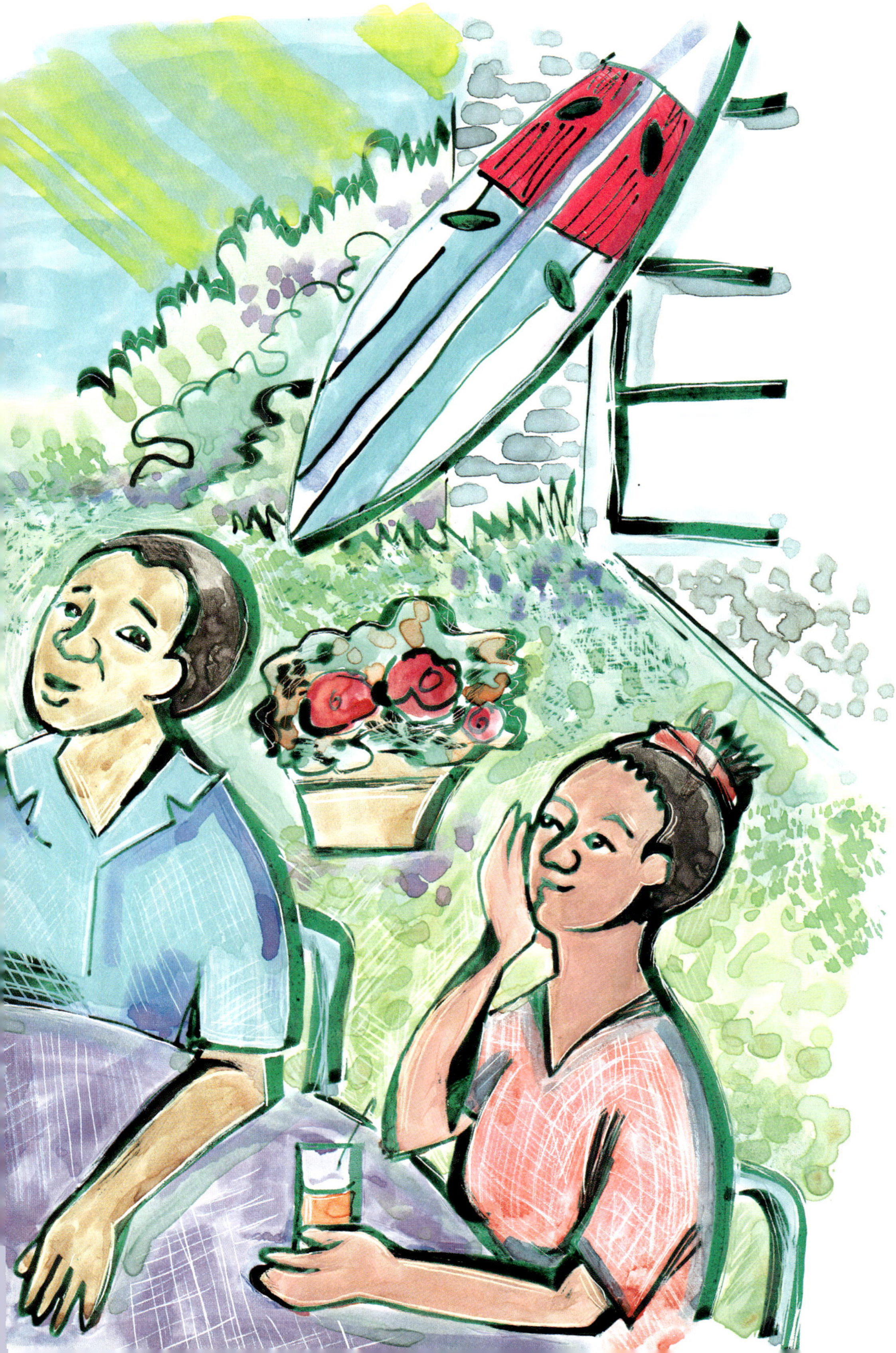

Focus Questions What are some of the most common ingredients in Indian cooking? Which Indian foods would you most like to eat?

Spice Up Your Day

by Ian Trevor

What is your favorite food? Do you eat a special snack after school? Can you name some of the popular foods you and your friends eat? These foods may be common in some households, but families in other parts of the world enjoy different types of foods as their most common meals.

India is a country in southern Asia. It is home to more than one billion people. Many Indians do not believe in eating animals. They do not eat animals for religious reasons or for ethical reasons (they do not feel it is the right thing to do). People who do not eat animals are called vegetarians.

You may be asking yourself, "What do vegetarians in India eat?" They actually have many food choices. In fact, Indian diets are becoming more popular in the United States as well.

On a typical day in many parts of India, children rise to the smells of their parents cooking a breakfast of potatoes, onions, yogurt, fresh fruit, tea, and coffee. Many spices are used in Indian cooking. A popular breakfast dish is called *khichri*. It is made with rice, lentils (the seeds of a plant similar to peas and beans), and spices. Other popular breakfast foods include rice pancakes filled with vegetables, rice noodles, and cakes made with rice and peas and served with bananas.

As children in India open their lunch bags, they find a bread called *naan*. Naan is soft, round, and flat. It is filled with many types of vegetables and sometimes cheese or yogurt to make a sandwich. People in India also might eat fresh salads, fruit, spicy potatoes, vegetable soups, and rice for lunch.

After a long day at school or at work, Indians welcome the aroma of spices coming from their homes. Before hitting the books, Indian children might enjoy some vegetarian snacks. One favorite is *batata vada*. You are probably familiar with dumplings, small balls of dough usually served in a broth. Batata vada is deep-fried potato dumplings . . . yum! Another favorite is crispy rice loops. No, this is not a breakfast cereal. Crispy rice loops are made from rice flour that is deep-fried into the shape of loops. Many people eat them with tea. As with other Indian recipes, many Indian snack recipes have been passed down from generation to generation.

But it is not a good idea to fill up on snacks. Many wonderful recipes await, and dinner is ready! A typical Indian dinner might include appetizers called *palak vada* and vegetable *bonda*. Palak vada is steamed spinach dumplings. Vegetable bonda is deep-fried vegetable dumplings. Salads made from carrots, cucumbers, pineapple, and mango are often on the menu as well.

Once again, rice, lentils, and vegetables make up many of the dinner recipes. Of course, they are blended with many different spices, some of them very hot! You may have heard of chili powder. It is also popular in many recipes in the United States. This is a common spice in Indian cooking along with some you may not have heard of—cardamom, cumin, turmeric, mustard seeds, and the curry leaf. A popular side dish on American menus is cottage cheese. Cottage cheese is also popular in India. It is used in many main dishes mixed with green peppers, black pepper, and spinach.

As in many different countries, the end of a day would not be complete without a sweet treat. Desserts in India include rice, carrot, and nut puddings. Many Indian desserts are made using nuts, coconut, pumpkin, and fruits such as pineapple and mango. One of the most popular desserts in India is *gajar ka halwa*. It is a carrot pudding made with nuts and other dried fruit.

These mouthwatering Indian dishes are accompanied by various beverages. Two popular drinks in India are the universal coffee and tea. However, Indian beverages are usually flavored with spices. A healthful Indian drink is *lassi*, which is made with yogurt. Chilled mangos and nuts make good shakes too. One Indian drink that has made its way to the United States is chai (chī). *Chai* is the Hindi word for "tea." Chai is a spiced milk tea and is more popular in India than coffee. The next time you visit a coffee shop, try the chai to enjoy a typical Indian beverage.

Vegetarians can be found in every country. Most recipes can be adapted to meet vegetarian requirements. But in no other nation is being a vegetarian as much a part of life as in India. Vegetarians and nonvegetarians can thank Indian cooks for inspiring some of the most delicious and healthful recipes in the world.

Focus Questions How is Mexico a land of contrasts? What pastimes are enjoyed there?

Mexico:
A Study in Contrasts

by Garrett McTavish

The Land

Mexico is, without a doubt, a land of contrasts. A trek across this country will prove this is true. There is snow on the "White Lady" volcano and 120°F temperatures in Baja. In the west, deserts are so barren they have been used as testing grounds for lunar landings. In the east, there are lush tropical rain forests.

In 1986 Mexico set aside 1.3 million acres for a biosphere reserve. This protected wildlife area is called Sian Ka'an, or "place where the sky is born." It includes rain forest, savanna, and coral reefs off the shore. The reserve is home to hundreds of species of animals, including jaguars, wild pigs, monkeys, parrots, crocodiles, and manatees. There are more than 1,200 kinds of plants. And there are more than twenty sites of Mayan ruins. Much of the reserve is restricted to scientific research, and it is now listed as a World Heritage Site. Yet the reserve also allows native people with ancestral ties to hunt, fish, and live on parts of the land.

A Mayan temple at Palenque in Mexico

Copper Canyon

In contrast to the below-sea-level reefs, Mexico's Sierra Madre mountains have peaks more than 12,000 feet high. Copper Canyon in Chihuahua is more than a mile deep and is more rugged than the Grand Canyon in the United States. Since the rail line has been completed, parts of the canyon can be seen from a train. The line uses 39 bridges and 86 tunnels to travel from sea level to more than 8,000 feet.

Past and Present

Like many countries, Mexico has a number of conflicts in its history. The ancient Mayan and Aztec people fought wars with the Spanish conquistadores who wanted their land. Today, however, the two groups are united. Sixty percent of more than 100 million people in Mexico are Mestizo, of both Native American and Spanish heritage.

Despite its past conflicts, Mexico is now also the place where a fragile insect is a protected species. Each November, thousands of monarch butterflies migrate here. Some come from as far away as Canada. These delicate insects fly seventy miles per day to winter where their ancestors wintered. Their life span is just a few months. It is the butterflies of the next generations who will return to the same areas. They land in large numbers on trees. Branches bend and even break from the weight of so many butterflies. The sound of their wings beating together in flight can be heard if one listens closely.

Art History

Contrasts characterize Mexican art history as well. Mexico provided the setting where two very different famous artists met and married. Diego Rivera believed art should serve the working people. He also felt art should be accessible to them. His huge murals show historical events and social problems. On the other hand, his wife, Frida Kahlo, painted small self-portraits. Her more portable work traveled to shows around the world. Kahlo's beginnings as an artist were also of a more personal nature; she taught herself to paint after she was involved in a terrible bus accident.

Anna Guevara

Sports

Mexico has many baseball and soccer teams. In fact, Mexico City alone has four soccer stadiums. There is, of course, a huge fan population. And Mexico has hosted the World Cup twice.

This is a country where male soccer players have been the superstars of the sports world. Now, however, three young women have begun to share the fame. Lorena Ochoa became the first Mexican woman to win a golf tournament as a paid player. Since then, many more people are playing golf. Songs have been written about the speed and grace of track star Anna Guevara. And Soraya Jimenez's Olympic gold medal for lifting weights is a source of pride for all of Mexico.

Work and Home

Most Mexican school lessons are taught in lectures. There are also many rules in the classroom. In contrast to this strict approach in school, the work day contains a long midday meal break. This meal is called a *comida*, which means "food," "meal," or "lunch" in Spanish. It starts at one or two o'clock and lasts at least two hours. Work resumes around five o'clock in the late afternoon.

Life in Mexico centers around the many varieties of family groups. Children most often live at home until they are married, and, for many, spending quality time with family and friends is the first priority. As a result, it is not unusual for three or four generations of a family to gather for meals on a regular basis. In a land of many contrasts, families and friends in Mexico share the common ground of their lives together.

Focus Questions What is troubling Hendrika? What does she realize about herself?

Touring the Amsterdam Canal

by Sophie Millet
illustrated by Marcy Ramsey

It was a cold, overcast morning in the capital city of Amsterdam. The weather in the Netherlands is usually mild, and it rarely snows, but this day was an exception. Flakes had started to drift from the gray sky a few hours earlier.

This was the kind of day that made it hard for Hendrika Van der Berg to throw off the covers, gather her books, and head off to school. Hendrika had a long day ahead of her, and after school she had to ride to her part-time job. *At least riding the canal boat is fun*, she thought, as she forced herself out of bed.

The Netherlands has more than sixty canals. They were built in order to drain water from the land and make it usable and livable. The canals are also an excellent means of transportation. Thousands of tourists visit Amsterdam every year, and many of them want to tour the city by canal boat. Hendrika's job was to lead these tours. In fact, she was ideal for this position. Always outgoing, she spoke Dutch, English, and French and could communicate with many different visitors.

Hendrika had been a tour guide for almost a year now. She was getting close to completing her formal education, however, and needed to decide on a career. Her parents continually asked her what her future plans were. But it seemed she already had enough to think about with final exams looming, the demands of hockey and soccer, and, of course, her after-school job. She thought about the job a lot, actually. She genuinely liked showing off her city to visitors. The canal boat passed both historical and commercial places. The popular cafés, restaurants, and trendy boutiques were interesting, but Hendrika preferred to speak to tourists about the many museums and landmarks from the past.

Hendrika threw on her heavier coat, grabbed her books and her bicycle, and headed for school. Like many people in Amsterdam, Hendrika rode her bicycle everywhere. *It's definitely cold out here today*, she thought to herself as she pedaled along. *If it gets even colder, maybe the ice will freeze, and there will be no tours today. Then I can go ice-skating!*

As the final school bell sounded, though, Hendrika saw that it had warmed up during the day. Her passengers would be waiting if she did not hurry. She jumped on her bike and made her way to her tour boat. She got there in plenty of time to check in with the tour director, make sure her boat was neat and clean, and double-check that her microphone was working. She no longer needed a script to get her through the tour; she knew it all by heart.

It was a full boat this day. Hendrika would probably have to speak Dutch, English, and French. She was about forty-five minutes into her hour-and-a-half tour when the boat cruised by one of the most popular spots on the route—the house of Anne Frank.

Frank was born in Germany in the late 1920s. She was still a child when World War II broke out and the Nazis began their persecution of the Jews. Being of Jewish faith, Frank's family had migrated to the Netherlands. When the Nazis occupied the Netherlands, the family went into hiding in the annex of an office building in Amsterdam.

The annex was a secret area of the building that became the family's home for two years. Eventually they were betrayed, discovered, and sent to concentration camps where Frank and everyone in her family except her father perished. Later, a diary Frank had kept was discovered in the annex. She had recorded detailed descriptions of the family's years in hiding, along with other stories. The diary was made into a book, *The Diary of Anne Frank*, and later a play. The annex where the family hid is now a museum.

Hendrika was a bit of a history buff. Not all tour guides knew as many historic details as she did. She could see the deep and sorrowful expressions on her passengers' faces as she described the Frank family's difficult life during World War II. On this particular day, a little boy seemed overly fascinated by the story of Anne Frank. Hendrika was somewhat surprised by the emotion he expressed and the heartfelt questions he asked. Hendrika spent some extra time with him, and they even chatted for a while at the end of the tour. Hendrika could tell how much the little boy appreciated her attention.

"That's it!" Hendrika said as she jumped back on her bicycle. The experience with the little boy had turned on a light in Hendrika's head. She loved people, history, and talking. She knew what career she wanted to pursue. She raced over to the café where her best friend, Kalie, worked to tell her the news. Hendrika's family, too, would be proud of her decision. She wanted to be a history teacher.

Focus Questions What are the steps of the Tuareg tea ceremony? Why is the ceremony important?

Tea with Friends

by Dorothea Nixon

It is another sweltering afternoon on the edge of the great Sahara Desert. The relentless sun bakes the earth. A group of village elders wrapped in vivid cotton fabrics gathers under the shade of a mango tree. Their movements are slow in the oppressive heat. As the men talk idly, one fans the hot coals in a small clay stove. Another pours tea leaves into a metal teapot. An age-old but daily ceremony has begun.

For the Tuareg people of Mali and other countries of northern and western Africa, the making of tea—besides offering refreshment—is an important social ritual. Each day across bustling cities and rural villages, groups of men or women meet to brew this hot drink and to chat. The tea ceremony has many steps and provides ample time for a good conversation.

To begin the Tuareg tea ceremony, the tea maker lights the coals or wood of a small stove. While the stove is heating, he or she puts a small mound of green tea leaves, along with a little bit of water, into a metal teapot. The teapot has a long spout, a hinged lid, and a handle. It is then placed on the stove so the tea can begin brewing.

Next, when the water in the teapot has begun to boil, the tea maker uses a small glass to pour more water into the pot. After three glassfuls are added, the pot is put back on the stove to boil again. Then up to one whole glassful of white sugar is added to the pot for sweetening.

Next comes the showiest part of the tea ceremony. The tea maker pours tea from the pot into the glass with a flourish, raising the pot higher and higher as he or she pours and then lowering it back over the glass. This impressive pouring method is a vital part of the ceremony and is done without fail. The tea in the glass then quickly goes back in the teapot. The transfer of tea from the pot to the glass and back is repeated several times to help brew the tea. It also brings the tea to a drinkable temperature.

When the tea is ready, it is served in the small glasses used for the brewing process. The pot will produce three glassfuls of strong, sweet tea. The Tuareg say the first glass represents the strength of the young. The second stands for the smoothness of middle age, and the third glass recalls the sweet taste of old age.

It is easy to see that tea and tea making are at the heart of everyday life for these people, for tea making gives them time to reflect and to converse. It also gives them time to practice the precise movements of their ancestors. And in the heat of the day, it is nice to rest in the shade and share something sweet with friends.

Focus Questions What are some of the sights and sounds of Carnaval? How does Carnaval help Brazilians celebrate their heritage?

Brazil's Big Party

by Justin Blanco

Since the early nineteenth century, Brazilians have been journeying once a year to the city of Rio de Janeiro to samba and celebrate life at Carnaval, Brazil's largest festival. This four-day holiday, often in late February, brings the country's people together to pay tribute to their heritage and diversity. It also gives them a chance to have loads of fun.

The most popular attraction of Carnaval is the samba parades. These parades have become so large that in the 1980s Brazil asked the native architect Oscar Niemeyer to build an outdoor arena to host them. The Sambadrome is one of the world's largest amphitheaters. It features box and bleacher seats and, of course, a long, white road running through the center. It offers plenty of room for the floats, bands, and costumed dancers to move and dance. Carnaval has become so popular that the event is televised live around the world. The parades take place over several days and are considered some of the greatest shows on Earth.

Brazil's most famous style of music and dance, the samba, comes from its West African heritage. The dance is powered by catchy drumbeats that make toe tapping irresistible. The samba is so popular that Brazil has many schools called *escolas de samba* devoted to it. These schools work all year on their music and dance routines for the samba parades. Then they compete for prizes in the Sambadrome. The competition between schools is fierce and dates back to the 1930s.

Carnaval offers a snapshot of Brazil's varied population. The revelers include descendants of the land's native people and the Portuguese who colonized Brazil. Also present are the descendants of Africans brought over to work the land. The sounds of Portuguese and other European languages mingle in the air. Different neighborhoods of people dress in themed outfits and proceed through the streets to the beat of their own music. The dances, drums, costumes, and traditions on display during Carnaval represent every ancestral group that has touched Brazilian culture.

Many believe the tradition of Carnaval comes from the Portuguese custom of pranks called *entrudo*. In the seventeenth and eighteenth centuries, entrudo involved a playful throwing of water, mud, and flour on unsuspecting passersby. Carnaval also has origins in the festive Brazilian masquerade balls of the nineteenth century. These dances, in which the people wore elaborate costumes and masks, are still a part of the celebration today.

Visitors to Carnaval will find themselves on constantly crowded streets. The smell of spicy, grilled Brazilian beef teases their taste buds. A powerful samba beat propels their feet to their next destinations. And behind a sea of ornate masks, partygoers of all situations and backgrounds leave their cares behind. That is Carnaval's greatest contribution. It joins all of Brazil's people in a celebration of life and culture that is unmatched anywhere else in the world.

Focus Questions What do you know about the stars? Does stargazing sound like an interesting pastime?

African Night

by Susan Scott Sutton
illustrated by Ken Perkins

Do you know the night as I do?

Cool earth cradling bare back,
Soft breeze fanning sun-burnished skin,
Heart free, soul soaring
    to endless sky;
Deep, wide darkness
    flashing diamonds . . .
The African night is full of stars.

Do you know the stars as I do?

Hen lays her eggs in one eternal cluster,
The Old Woman dances with her Children Three,
Big Giraffe, Little Giraffe mark their places
    while
The Way of the Elephant trails
    a dusty streak across the sky.

Do you know the night as I do?
The African night full of stars.

Pastimes

Poetry Reflections

These questions can help you think about the poem. Write your answers. Then talk about them with a partner.
- In the beginning of the poem, the speaker is describing a pastime he or she enjoys. What is it? How do you know?
- The speaker seems to see a hen, an old woman, and giraffes in the night sky. What is he or she really seeing?
- Do you ever gaze at the stars? What do you see? Is your experience like what the speaker has described?

Unit 6

Reading Reflections

These questions can help you think about the stories you read. Write your answers. Then talk about them with a partner.

Focus on the Facts

- In "Tea with Friends," why do the Tuaregs practice the tea ceremony?
- Think about "Mexico: A Study in Contrasts." Which animal migrates many miles to winter in Mexico? How many miles does it travel a day?
- Think about "Spice Up Your Day." Name three types of Indian foods that use rice.

Focus on the Stories

- In "The Very Best Sport," Cliff thinks through what sport he is most passionate about. He worries that his parents will not understand. Who considers a life passion in another story? Is that character worried about others' reactions? Why or why not?
- Brazilians in "Brazil's Big Party" celebrate their heritage through Carnaval. Think about the other stories. How do people in another culture honor their own traditions?
- What sport is popular in both Mexico and Barbados, according to "The Very Best Sport" and "Mexico: A Study in Contrasts"? Do you think it is as popular in the United States?

Pastimes

Focus on the Theme
- Meals and special foods are an important part of many of this unit's stories. Why do you think eating special food is a popular pastime in many countries? Describe one traditional food your family enjoys.
- In "Touring the Amsterdam Canal," Hendrika thinks about what she likes to do. It helps her decide on a future career. What types of activities do you like? Do they relate to any careers?
- Sports, art, and dance are important parts of many cultures. Describe your favorite type of sport, art, or dance. Why do you like it?

Glossary

Pronunciation Key

a as in **a**t	**o** as in **o**x	**ou** as in **ou**t	**ch** as in **ch**air
ā as in l**a**te	**ō** as in r**o**se	**u** as in **u**p	**hw** as in w**h**ich
â as in c**a**re	**ô** as in b**ou**ght and r**aw**	**ū** as in **u**se	**ng** as in ri**ng**
ä as in f**a**ther		**ûr** as in t**ur**n, g**er**m, l**ear**n, f**ir**m, w**or**k	**sh** as in **sh**op
e as in s**e**t	**oi** as in c**oi**n		**th** as in **th**in
ē as in m**e**	**o͝o** as in b**oo**k		**t͟h** as in **th**ere
i as in **i**t	**o͞o** as in t**oo**	**ə** as in **a**bout, chick**e**n, penc**i**l, cann**o**n, circ**u**s	**zh** as in trea**s**ure
ī as in k**i**te	**or** as in f**or**m		

The mark (´) is placed after a syllable with a heavy accent, as in chicken (chik´ ən).

The mark (`) after a syllable shows a lighter accent, as in disappear (dis´ ə pēr`).

A

accompanied (ə kum´ pə nēd) *v.* Past tense of **accompany:** To go along with.

account (ə kount´) *n.* A report of something.

adapted (ə dapt´ ed) *v.* Past tense of **adapt:** To change in order to make more suitable.

allies (a´ līz) *n.* Plural form of **ally:** A person or group joined with another to do something.

alternative (ôl tûr´ nə tiv) *n.* One of two or more things that may be chosen.

amateur (am´ ə chər) *adj.* Done by people without much experience or skill.

amphitheaters (am´ fə thē´ ə tərz) *n.* Plural form of **amphitheater:** A round or oval building with rows of seats that is used for sports or other public events.

ample (am´ pəl) *adj.* More than enough.

appetizers (ap´ ə tī´ zərz) *n.* Plural form of **appetizer:** A small snack served before a meal.

aroma (ə rō´ mə) *n.* A smell.

artisans (är´ ti zanz) *n.* Plural form of **artisan:** Someone skilled at a craft.

ascended (ə send´ ed) *v.* Past tense of **ascend:** To move upward.

assented (ə sent´ ed) *v.* Past tense of **assent:** To agree.

associated (ə sō´ shē āt´ ed) *v.* Past tense of **associate:** To connect with.

atlas (at´ ləs) *n.* A book of maps.

attempted (ə tempt´ ed) *v.* Past tense of **attempt:** To try.

auditorium (ô´ di tor´ ē əm) *n.* A large room where people can gather.

256

Glossary

B

bamboo (bam bōō´) *n.* A plant with long woody stems.

banjo (ban´ jō) *n.* A musical instrument with a round body, a long neck, and five strings.

barred (bärd) *v.* Past tense of **bar:** To keep out.

barren (bâr´ ən) *adj.* Having little or no plant life.

beverages (bev´ ər ij əz) *n.* Plural of **beverage:** A liquid for drinking.

blues (blōōz) *n.* Music that sounds sad and has a jazz rhythm.

blur (blûr) *n.* Something dim or difficult to see.

boutiques (bōō tēks´) *n.* Plural form of **boutique:** A small shop.

brochure (brō shûr´) *n.* A booklet that informs people about something.

broth (broth) *n.* A thin soup made by boiling meat or vegetables in water.

C

calcium (kal´ sē əm) *n.* A chemical element needed by bones and teeth.

calisthenics (kal´ əs the´ niks) *n.* A group of exercises for the body.

cartilage (kär´ tə lij) *n.* A strong, flexible material that forms parts of the body.

cautionary (kô´ shən âr´ ē) *adj.* Describing a danger.

chrysanthemums (krə san´ thə məmz) *n.* Plural form of **chrysanthemum:** A round, brightly colored flower.

circulate (sûr´ kyə lāt´) *v.* To cause to move around.

coarse (kors) *adj.* Thick and rough.

coiled (koild) *v.* Past tense of **coil:** To wind round and round.

colony (kol´ ə nē´) *n.* A group of similar animals or plants that live together.

compass (kum´ pəs) *n.* A device for finding directions.

complex (käm pleks´) *adj.* Difficult to understand or do.

composed (kəm pōzd´) *v.* Past tense of **compose:** To put together; create.

comprised (kəm prīzd´) *v.* Past tense of **comprise:** To be made up of.

contemplate (kon´ təm plāt´) *v.* To carefully and thoughtfully consider.

continent (kon´ tə nənt) *n.* One of the seven major land masses of Earth.

conversation (kon´ vər sā´ shən) *n.* A talk with someone.

converse (kən vûrs´) *v.* To talk together.

cumbersome (kum´ bər səm) *adj.* Hard to carry because of weight, shape, or size.

Glossary

cunning

cunning (kun´ ing) *n.* A cleverness at fooling others.

current (kûr´ ənt) *n.* A stream or flow of water or air.

D

debilitated (di bil´ ə tāt´ ed) *v.* Past tense of **debilitate:** To weaken.

dejectedly (di jek´ tid lē) *adv.* In a sad or depressed way.

delicacies (del´ i kə sēz) *n.* Plural form of **delicacy:** Something good to eat that is thought to be rare.

densely (dens´ lē) *adv.* Close together.

detect (di tekt´) *v.* To find out or notice.

devised (di vīzd´) *v.* Past tense of **devise:** To think up or come up with.

digestion (dī jes´ chən) *n.* The process of breaking down food so it can be used by the body.

dismayed (dis mād´) *v.* Past tense of **dismay:** To shock or surprise.

dispose (di spōz´) *v.* To get rid of.

distinguished (di stin´ gwishd) *adj.* Famous for something achieved.

documentary (doc´ ū ment´ ə rē) *n.* A film or a television program using pictures or interviews with real people to present real events.

drifted (drift´ ed) *v.* Past tense of **drift:** To move because of the flow of air or water.

expertise

duct (dukt) *n.* A tube or a pipe that carries air or water.

durable (dûr´ ə bəl) *adj.* Able to last a long time despite much use.

dynamic (dī nam´ ik) *adj.* Having or showing a lot of energy.

E

ecstatic (ek stat´ ik) *adj.* Very happy.

elegant (el´ i gənt) *adj.* Rich and fine in quality.

elements (el´ ə mənts) *n.* Plural form of **element:** One of the parts that something is made of.

emigrated (em´ ə grāt´ ed) *v.* Past tense of **emigrate:** To leave one place or country to live in another.

enlisted (en list´ ed) *v.* Past tense of **enlist:** To join the armed forces.

ensure (en shūr´) *v.* To make sure of something.

exaggerated (eg zaj´ ə rāt´ ed) *v.* Past tense of **exaggerate:** To make something seem larger or greater than it is.

exceptional (ek sep´ shən əl) *adj.* Not ordinary; unusual.

expertise (eks´ pûr tēs´) *n.* Detailed knowledge about something that comes from training and experience.

Glossary

fiber

F

fiber (fī´ bər) *n.* A strand of nerve tissue.

flavored (flā´ vərd) *v.* Past tense of **flavor**: To give taste to.

fleet (flēt) *n.* A group of ships led by one person.

flung (flung) *v.* Past tense of **fling**: To throw with force; hurl.

footage (fo͝ot´ ij) *n.* A length or an amount of film used for movies or television.

formulated (fôr´ myu̅ lāt´ ed) *v.* Past tense of **formulate**: To come up with; devise.

fragrant (frā´ grənt) *adj.* Having a sweet or pleasing smell.

fuel (fū´ əl) *n.* Something that provides power.

funds (fundz) *n.* Plural form of **fund**: A sum of money that is readily available.

G

gaping (gāp´ ing) *v.* A form of **gape**: To be opened wide.

garb (gärb) *n.* A style of clothing.

gear (gēr) *n.* Equipment used for a purpose.

generations (jen´ ər ā´ shənz) *n.* Plural form of **generation**: A group of people born around the same time.

hulls

genuinely (jen´ yə win lē) *adv.* Truly; honestly.

glanced (glansd) *v.* Past tense of **glance**: To look quickly.

glands (glandz) *n.* Plural form of **gland**: A body part that takes substances from the blood and makes them into chemicals the body uses or gives off.

glimpsed (glimpsd) *v.* Past tense of **glimpse**: To see for a moment.

H

harmonica (här mon´ i kə) *n.* A musical instrument that consists of a small case with slots that are blown into.

harp (härp) *n.* A musical instrument with strings that are plucked.

hesitation (hez´ i tā´ shən) *n.* A delay or a pause because of uncertainty.

hobble (hob´ əl) *v.* To limp.

hoisted (hoist´ ed) *v.* Past tense of **hoist**: To lift or pull up.

honorary (on´ ə rär´ ē) *adj.* Given as an honor or award.

horizon (hə rī´ zən) *n.* The line in the distance where the land or the sea seems to meet the sky.

hovered (huv´ ərd) *v.* Past tense of **hover**: To stay in the air, flying above one place.

hulls (hulz) *n.* Plural form of **hull**: The body of a ship.

Glossary

humanitarian

humanitarian (hyū ma´ nə ter´ ē ən) *n.* A person who cares about and tries to help people.

I

ideal (ī dē´ əl) *adj.* Just what one hopes for; perfect.

idly (ī´ dəl ē) *adv.* In an inactive way.

illustrious (il us´ trē əs) *adj.* Well respected and famous.

impact (im´ pakt) *n.* A strong effect.

impulses (im´ puls ez) *n.* Plural form of **impulse:** A wave of energy that moves through the body's nerves.

inauguration (i nô´ gyə rā´ shən) *n.* The ceremony of putting a person in office.

inquisitive (in kwiz´ i tiv) *adj.* Curious or eager for knowledge.

instrumental (in´ strə ment´ əl) *adj.* Played with musical instruments.

intense (in tens´) *adj.* Very strong; extreme.

L

lilt (lilt) *n.* A rhythmic swing or flow.

lint (lint) *n.* A small fuzz made from fabric fibers.

looming (lōōm´ ing) *v.* A form of **loom:** To appear as something large or dangerous in the future.

migrated

lunged (lunjd) *v.* Past tense of **lunge:** To move forward suddenly.

lush (lush) *adj.* Thick, rich, and plentiful.

lyrics (li´ riks) *n.* The words of a song.

M

majestic (mə jes´ tik) *adj.* Having greatness.

majesty (maj´ əs tē) *n.* Grandness or splendor.

maneuvers (mə nōō´ vərs) *n.* Plural form of **maneuver:** A planned movement.

mascot (mas´ kot) *n.* The symbol of a team thought to bring good luck.

massive (mas´ iv) *adj.* Extremely large.

mast (mast) *n.* The pole on a ship that holds the sails.

matinee (mat´ ə nā´) *n.* A movie shown in the afternoon.

melodies (mel´ ə dēz) *n.* Plural form of **melody:** A series of musical notes; tune.

membrane (mem´ brān) *n.* A thin layer of tissue.

mentor (men´ tər) *n.* A trusted guide.

merchants (mûr´ chəntz) *n.* Plural form of **merchant:** Someone who buys and sells products.

migrated (mī´ grāt´ ed) *v.* Past tense of **migrate:** To move from one place to another.

Glossary

mingle (min´ gəl) *v.* To mix.

modern (mod´ ərn) *adj.* Having to do with the present time.

modest (mod´ ist) *adj.* Simple.

monitor (mon´ i tər) *v.* To watch over something.

mortal (mor´ təl) *n.* A person; a human being.

mounted (mount´ ed) *v.* Past tense of **mount:** To climb up.

movement (mōōv´ mənt) *n.* A part of a long musical piece.

mucous (myū´ kəs) *adj.* Containing or covered with a slimy substance produced by the body.

muffled (muf´ əld) *adj.* Softened or muted.

N

naturalist (nach´ ər əl ist) *n.* A person who studies nature.

navigators (nav´ ə gā´ tərz) *n.* Plural form of **navigator:** A person who explores by ship.

nimble (nim´ bəl) *adj.* Moving lightly and quickly.

nutrients (nōō´ trē əntz) *n.* Plural form of **nutrient:** Something that is needed for life and growth.

O

offensive (ə fen´ siv) *adj.* Causing anger or unhappiness.

oppressive (ə pres´ iv) *adj.* Troubling or causing a burden.

ornate (or nāt´) *adj.* Having a lot of decoration.

outsmarting (out smart´ ing) *v.* A form of **outsmart:** To be more clever than.

overcast (ō´ vər kast´) *adj.* Cloudy.

P

panel (pan´ əl) *n.* A group of people gathered to judge something.

partake (pär tāk´) *v.* To have something to eat or drink.

particles (pär´ ti kəlz) *n.* Plural form of **particle:** A very small piece of something.

persecution (pûr si kyū´ shən) *n.* Cruel treatment over time.

petition (pə ti´ shən) *n.* A formal request made to a person in authority.

physician (fə zish´ ən) *n.* A doctor.

plagued (plāgd) *v.* Past tense of **plague:** To trouble or annoy.

podium (pō´ dē əm) *n.* A small platform or stand used by a public speaker to hold notes or books.

ports (ports) *n.* Plural form of **port:** A place by the water where ships and boats can dock.

Glossary

prejudice

prejudice (prej´ ə dis) *n.* The unfair treatment or dislike of a particular group.

premiered (pri mē´ ərd) *v.* Past tense of **premiere:** To have a first public performance.

prim (prim) *adj.* Proper; formal.

priority (prī or´ ə tē) *n.* Something that is made to come first.

prompted (prompt´ ed) *v.* Past tense of **prompt:** To cause to do something.

propels (prə pelz´) *v.* A form of **propel:** To cause to move forward.

prospects (pros´ pekts) *n.* Plural form of **prospect:** Something looked forward to.

R

rapped (rapt) *v.* Past tense of **rap:** To knock loudly.

redeem (ri dēm´) *v.* To make up for.

reefs (rēfs) *n.* Plural form of **reef:** A ridge of sand, rock, or coral on or near the ocean's surface.

reflect (ri flekt´) *v.* To think carefully.

regarded (ri gärd´ ed) *v.* Past tense of **regard:** To look at closely.

regretting (ri gret´ ing) *v.* A form of **regret:** To feel sorry about.

reluctant (ri luk´ tənt) *adj.* Not willing to do something.

remote (ri mōt´) *adj.* Far away.

shanty

repulsed (ri pəlsd´) *v.* Past tense of **repulse:** To cause a feeling of dislike or disgust.

requirements (ri kwīr´ mənts) *n.* Plural form of **requirement:** Something that is needed.

reserve (ri zûrv´) *n.* Land used for a special purpose.

respected (ri spekt´ ed) *adj.* Treated with high regard; admired.

restricted (ri strikt´ ed) *v.* Past tense of **restrict:** To keep within limits.

resumes (ri zo͞omz´) *v.* A form of **resume:** To start again after stopping.

revelers (rev´ ə lərz) *n.* Plural form of **reveler:** A person who takes part in a party.

revolves (ri volvz´) *v.* A form of **revolve:** To depend on.

S

savanna (sə van´ ə) *n.* A flat, grassy land with few trees.

scoffed (skoft) *v.* Past tense of **scoff:** To show disrespect for.

score (skor) *n.* Written or printed music.

scurrying (skûr´ ē ing) *v.* A form of **scurry:** To move around quickly.

sensitive (sen´ si tiv) *adj.* Able to react to a certain thing.

shanty (shan´ tē) *n.* A small, simply built hut.

Glossary

shuddered (shud´ ərd) *v.* Past tense of **shudder:** To tremble suddenly.

sly (slī) *adj.* Clever and crafty.

smug (smug) *adj.* Very pleased with oneself.

sod (sod) *n.* A clump of grass and dirt; turf.

solos (sō´ lōz) *n.* Plural form of **solo:** A musical piece played or sung by only one person or featuring one person.

specialists (spesh´ ə lists) *n.* Plural form of **specialist:** Someone who is best at or knows the most about a particular thing.

stammered (stam´ ərd) *v.* Past tense of **stammer:** To speak with difficulty.

startled (star´ təld) *adj.* Surprised or frightened.

stir (stûr) *n.* A burst of excitement.

stooped (stōōpt) *adj.* Bent over.

superior (sə pēr´ ē ər) *adj.* Higher, greater, or better.

suspicion (sə spish´ ən) *n.* The act of thinking that something is possible.

sweltering (swel´ tər ing) *adj.* Very hot.

T

temporary (tem´ pə rer´ ē) *adj.* Lasting for a short time.

tenacity (tə na´ sə tē) *n.* The state of being persistent or of holding tight to something.

tenement house (ten´ ə mənt hous) *n.* An apartment house.

thorough (thûr´ ō) *adj.* Leaving nothing out.

touch (tuch) *n.* A small amount.

tragic (traj´ ik) *adj.* Very sad or dreadful.

transparent (trans pâr´ ənt) *adj.* Clear, so that light can pass through.

trenches (trench´ əz) *n.* Plural form of **trench:** A long, narrow ditch.

trend (trend) *n.* A direction or course that seems to be followed.

tribute (tri´ byūt) *n.* Something done to show thanks or respect.

trill (tril) *n.* A quivering sound in music.

tuning (tōōn´ ing) *v.* A form of **tune:** To fix a musical instrument so that it plays notes of the right pitch.

U

ukulele (ū´ kə lā´ lē) *n.* A small guitar popular in Hawaii.

V

vantage point (van´ tij point) *n.* A place that provides a wide view of something.

vast (vast) *adj.* Covering a large space.

vertebrae (vûr´ tə brā´) *n.* Plural form of **vertebra:** One of the small bones that make up the backbone.

Glossary

vessels

vessels (ves´ əlz) *n.* Plural form of **vessel:** A tube in the body for carrying blood.

vital (vī´ təl) *adj.* Very important.

vitamins (vī´ tə minz) *n.* Plural form of **vitamin:** A substance needed for good health.

voyages (voi´ i jez) *n.* Plural form of **voyage:** A long journey by air or sea.

W

waltzes (wôlts´ əz) *n.* Plural form of **waltz:** A ballroom dance in triple time or the music for this dance.

wits (wits) *n.* Plural form of **wit:** The ability to think and understand.